THE IRISH POUND 1797–1826

THE IRISH POUND 1797–1826

A reprint of the Report of the Committee of 1804 of the British House of Commons on the condition of the Irish currency

Edited by

FRANK WHITSON FETTER

Routledge
Taylor & Francis Group
LONDON AND NEW YORK

First published in 1955 by
Routledge
2 Park Square, Milton Park, Abingdon, Oxfordshire OX14 4RN
711 Third Avenue, New York, NY 10017

First issued in paperback 2014

Routledge is an imprint of the Taylor and Francis Group, an informa business

British Library Cataloguing in Publication Data
A CIP catalogue record for this book
is available from the British Library

The Irish Pound 1797–1826
ISBN 0-415-38211-4 (volume)
ISBN 0-415-37850-8 (subset)
ISBN 0-415-28619-0 (set)

ISBN 13: 978-1-138-87982-9 (pbk)
ISBN 13: 978-0-415-38211-3 (hbk)

Routledge Library Editions: Economic History

THE IRISH POUND
1797–1826

A Reprint of the Report of the Committee of 1804
of the British House of Commons
on the Condition of the Irish Currency

WITH SELECTIONS FROM THE MINUTES
OF EVIDENCE PRESENTED TO THE COMMITTEE

AND

AN INTRODUCTION BY

FRANK WHITSON FETTER

George Allen and Unwin Ltd
RUSKIN HOUSE · MUSEUM STREET · LONDON

First published in 1955

CONTENTS

APPENDICES

CHARTS

PREFACE

THE Bullion Report of 1810 has had a popular fame and an influence on economic policy unequalled by any other public document on monetary problems. The reputation of the Bullion Report, and its association, in part legendary, with the name of David Ricardo, has overshadowed the earlier British Parliamentary Report of 1804 from "The Committee on The Circulating Paper, the Specie, and The Current Coin of Ireland." This Report contains a large part of the doctrine later incorporated in the Bullion Report on the relation between monetary and banking policy, prices, international payments, specie premium, and exchange rates, but applied to a somewhat different setting—the exchange situation between independent monetary systems in the same political sovereignty—and discussed in a more concise and realistic way than was done in the Bullion Report. Six of the members of the Bullion Committee had been members of the Irish Committee; two other members of the Bullion Committee, John Leslie Foster and Henry Parnell, although not members of the Irish Committee, had in 1804 participated in the public controversy over the fluctuations of the Irish exchange; and Francis Horner, the Chairman of the Bullion Committee, had followed closely the activities of the Committee of 1804 and possibly had some influence on the members of the Committee. The Irish Report was frequently cited in the pamphlet literature of the time, and in Parliamentary debate, and the Bullion Report made an extended reference to the Report of the Irish Committee and discussed in detail the exchange situation between Ireland and England.

The Bullion Report has been reprinted many times, and in some one of its editions is readily available to economists. But the Irish Report is today a scarce document, known first hand to comparatively few economists and available only in the larger libraries. I hope that this reprint of the Report and of portions of the Minutes of Evidence, set against the historical background, will not only be of interest to the student of monetary theory and of monetary history, but also help to give perspective on some present day problems of monetary and exchange policy, particularly in the countries of the sterling area.

It is doubtful whether any other British Parliamentary Report ever went through as many official editions as did the Irish Currency Report: in all five Parliamentary editions representing four separate printings. The original report of 1804 was published both as a Commons and as a Lords document, identical except for the title page; it was reprinted in 1810 by the Commons in connection with the investigation of the Bullion

Committee; it was reprinted in 1826, both as a Commons and as a Lords document, in connection with the Parliamentary investigations of the circulation of promissory notes in Ireland and Scotland. All of the editions include the Minutes of Evidence and the Appendix of Accounts.

A collation of the four printings reveals only differences in capitalization, punctuation and spelling, marginal references, and a few misprints. As the Commons edition of 1826 is the one most frequently available in libraries, and the one usually used by economists who have cited the Report, I have followed the text of that edition, except for the correction of three obvious misprints where I have restored the wording of the original edition: the substitution of "there" for "their" on p. 6, line 15, of the Commons edition of 1826; of "The place of the gold withdrawn" for "The place with the gold withdrawn" on p. 8, lines 4 and 5; and of "county" for "country" on p. 15, line 22.

A large part of the material used in editing this Report was collected while I was on a fellowship of the John Simon Guggenheim Memorial Foundation, and aid from the Committee on Research Funds of the Graduate School of Northwestern University made possible the completion of the work. Since I started this study so many persons have given me help, and so many libraries have extended privileges, that any attempt to indicate all of my obligations would run to undue length, and undoubtedly would, through oversight, be incomplete. I must, however, express my particular indebtedness to the Goldsmiths' Library of the University of London, and to the Kress Library of Business and Economics at Harvard University, for their continued courtesies in making available their rich resources. Professor Arthur H. Cole, Professor F. A. Hayek, Professor Virgil B. Heltzel, Professor Lloyd W. Mints, and Professor R. S. Sayers read the manuscript at some stage in its preparation, and I have benefited from their suggestions, although I have not always followed them. I am greatly indebted to Mr. J. K. Horsefield for his searching and exhaustive criticism of an earlier draft of the Introduction, and for his help in clarifying some troublesome points on banking practices and exchange rates in the Restriction period.

FRANK WHITSON FETTER

Northwestern University
December 22, 1953

INTRODUCTION

INTRODUCTION

INTRODUCTION

WHEN the Bank of England suspended specie payments in February, 1797, Ireland had a separate monetary system, with the specie value of the Irish pound 12/13ths of the specie value of the British pound. The notes of the Bank of Ireland, like the notes of the Bank of England, had been redeemable in specie, which in practice was gold, as a result of the fact that the mint ratio of approximately 1 : 15·2 set by the decree of 1717 had over-valued gold, and had driven out of circulation almost all full weight silver in England[1] and Ireland. Although the Bank of Ireland had not been subject to the run that had forced the Bank of England to suspend payments, the British Government also compelled the Bank of Ireland to stop redemption of its notes. This situation for the next twenty-four years under the Bank Restrictions, of independent inconvertible paper currencies within the same political sovereignty,[2] raised significant issues in monetary theory, as well as important questions of monetary policy. These developments after 1797 can best be understood against a background of the monetary and banking situation of Ireland before the Restriction.

EARLY MONETARY STANDARD OF IRELAND

At the time of the early English invasions Ireland had only a rudimentary monetary economy, and barter continued in most parts of the country long after the use of money had become general in England, and in rural districts in Ireland was common until well into the nineteenth century.[3] The English invasions brought in English coins, but through a development similar to that in the American colonies, whereby their pounds had a value different from the pounds of England, the monies

[1] I have throughout this Introduction, following a practice common in most of the contemporary discussions of the Irish exchange, generally used the term England to refer not only to England proper, but also to Great Britain.

[2] Previous to the Union of Great Britain and Ireland in 1801, the countries had separate Parliaments and separate laws. The controversy over exchange rate fluctuations between Ireland and England was practically all in the period after the Union.

[3] Edmund Campion, writing in 1571, said of the Irish: "... they exchange by commutation of wares for the most part, and have utterly no coyne stirring in any great Lords houses." *A Historie of Ireland.* Reproduced in Scholar's Facsimiles and Reprints (New York, 1940), p. 20. The slow progress of the monetary economy into the rural sections of Ireland is indicated by a similar statement of Edward Wakefield, over two centuries later: "In places, however, remote from towns, the exchange of commodities is carried on by tally payments, without the intervention of circulating medium, a circumstance which forms a striking difference between the state of Ireland and of England." *An Account of Ireland, Statistical and Political.* (London, 1812.) Vol. II, p. 17.

of Ireland, although called pounds, shillings and pence, were not equal to the English units. The situation previous to 1701 is not clear, but at least since 1689 gold and silver coins had passed in Ireland at a higher valuation than in England. A proclamation of 1701 had given the English shilling a valuation of 1s. 1d. Irish, and a proclamation of 1737, fixing the guinea, worth 21s. English, at 22s. 9d. Irish, had in effect tied together the English and Irish monetary systems on a gold basis, with 13 Irish units equal to 12 English units.[1] This situation continued up to the suspension of payments in 1797. Hence the exchanges were considered at par when the premium on English currency in terms of Irish currency was 8 1/3 %, and both in London and in Dublin it was customary to quote exchange on the basis of the number of Irish pounds in excess of 100 that exchanged for £100 English.

The real monetary problems of Ireland throughout most of the eighteenth century were those of the shortage of silver and copper coins. No Irish silver had been minted since 1649 and the silver circulation consisted almost exclusively of badly worn English coins. There were several mintings of copper for Ireland, including the Wood half-pence made famous by the satirical and not always technically accurate writings of Jonathan Swift, but at times large quantities of private brass tokens, and even private I. O. U.'s, were in circulation. James Simon wrote in 1749: "What silver is now left, is some English money, not worth melting, shilling pieces hardly worth nine pence or ten pence, and six-penny pieces not worth a groat."[2] A witness before the Committee of 1804, in answer to a question as to whether the silver coin in Ireland was inferior to that in England prior to the Restriction, replied: "It was ever since I knew the Silver Coin of Ireland."[3]

EARLY HISTORY OF IRISH BANKING

Bank note issues developed in Ireland in much the same way that they had developed in England, out of the giving of receipts by goldsmiths and others for money deposited with them, and as a sideline of trade and commerce. Before the establishment of the Bank of Ireland in 1783 all Irish note issuing agencies were unincorporated, practically free from

[1] This account of the establishment of the 13 to 12 ratio between the two currencies is based on the account in James Simon, *An Essay Towards an Historical Account of Irish Coins, and of the Currency of Foreign Monies in Ireland.* (Dublin, 1810.) [This is the reprint of a book originally published in 1749.] Pp. 56–57, 73–74.

[2] *Op. cit.*, p. 75.

[3] Thomas Thorpe Frank, p. 75. All citations of the Report of 1804, and of the Minutes of Evidence, are to the 1826 edition. Another witness, Jeremiah D'Olier, made substantially the same statement. P. 76.

control and supervision except as an incident of tax legislation. By the middle of the eighteenth century bank notes were widely used in Dublin,[1] but apparently there was little circulation of Dublin bank notes in the country, and any issue of bank notes outside of Dublin was on a very limited scale. As a result of a panic in 1754 all but two of the Dublin banks failed, and these two retired their notes, so that for a brief time no paper money circulated in Ireland.[2] Soon afterwards private banks again started to issue circulating paper in Dublin, and notes were also issued in some of the provincial cities. The North of Ireland, however, had almost no paper circulation until 1808. A bank was established in Belfast in 1752 but lasted only five years, and another Belfast bank established in 1784 closed its doors in 1798.

In 1783 the Bank of Ireland, the first incorporated bank in the country, opened under an exclusive charter which forbade any other company with over six partners from issuing circulating notes. Until 1799 there were no legal restrictions in Ireland on the issue, either by the Bank of Ireland or by private banks, of notes of small denominations. No accurate figures are available as to the number of private bankers in Ireland before 1797, or the amount of their issues, but a Dublin banker, John Claudius Beresford, testifying before the Committee of 1804,[3] believed that the issue of the Dublin private bankers was about £700,000 in 1797. In 1797 the Bank of Ireland had outstanding notes of less than £700,000,[4] most of which circulated in Dublin. As compared with a gold circulation estimated at about £5,000,000[5] in addition to the silver and copper coins, the bank note circulation of Ireland made up but a small fraction of the total means of payment in the country in 1797.

IRISH MONETARY AND BANKING SITUATION IN 1797

The Bank of Ireland, which had been established less than fifteen years at the time of the Restriction, held a different relationship to the other banks of Ireland than the Bank of England held to the other banks of Great Britain. Dublin was not a financial clearing house for the rest of

[1] William Colville, testifying before the Irish Currency Committee of 1804, said: "I remember perfectly well, that in 1753, the circulation of Paper in Dublin from the private Bankers was so general and extensive, that in receiving £.1,000, there was not £.10 of it in Gold at that time." P. 121.

[2] Testimony of William Colville, pp. 121–122.

[3] P. 92.

[4] Unless otherwise indicated, all references in this Introduction to the note issues of the Bank of Ireland include the Bank's post bills.

[5] Evidence of Thomas Thorpe Frank, p. 110; evidence of Jeremiah D'Olier, p. 91.

Ireland in the way that London was for Great Britain. Its relation to the rest of Ireland was more that of a large provincial English city to the surrounding countryside. There was no foreign exchange market in Dublin and all financial dealings with the continent cleared through London, except for very limited transactions with Portugal. Not only did Belfast deal directly with London, but apparently there was also some direct dealing between smaller Irish cities and London.[1]

Information on banking practices in Ireland in 1797 is meagre,[2] but it seems clear that Bank of Ireland funds did not have the reserve significance for the Irish banks that Bank of England funds had for British banks. There is no evidence that either the Dublin bankers or the country bankers kept balances with the Bank of Ireland. Irish banks, in addition to gold, held part of their reserves in Bank of Ireland notes, but they never regarded the Bank of Ireland as enjoying the special position that the Bank of England held in the British banking system, and the Bank of Ireland had much less control over the Irish banks than the Bank of England had over the British banks. The Bank of Ireland had by law a monopoly in Ireland comparable to that of the Bank of England in Great Britain, but the difference in the age of the two institutions and in banking practices in the two countries made functional relationships between the "Bank" and private banks quite different on the opposite sides of the Irish Sea. The Dublin bankers issued notes that circulated in competition in Dublin with Bank of Ireland notes; and Bank of Ireland notes, and to a limited degree the notes of the Dublin bankers, circulated in the country in competition with the issues of local banks.

Henry Thornton, with his rare combination of familiarity with the details of banking practice and the ability to appraise the larger significance of those details, said in the Parliamentary debate of 1804, shortly before the appointment of the Irish Currency Committee:

> "There was a material difference . . . between the banks of England and Ireland: In Ireland there was no bank that took upon itself to manage and regulate the circulation of the country; whereas, in England it was perfectly well known, that the Bank commanded the whole paper circulation of the metropolis, and regulated that of the kingdom."[3]

[1] A Cork newspaper in 1804 quoted the exchange on London in Dublin, Belfast, and Cork; the Committee of 1804, Appendix M, published figures for the London exchange rate in Belfast and Newry.

[2] Most of the direct evidence on the Irish banking situation in this period refers specifically to 1803 and 1804, but there is no reason to believe that the situation in 1797 was materially different.

[3] Hansard, First Series, Vol. I, February 13, 1804, p. 1090.

RESTRICTION OF SPECIE PAYMENTS

The immediate circumstances that forced the Bank of Ireland to suspend specie payments were different from those that had caused the English Bank Restriction. Ireland, probably because its economy was more tied up with agriculture, and its banking system less developed, had largely escaped the financial crisis that England had suffered in 1793. Although the Irish Government had substantial deficits after 1793 as a result of the war with France, the problems of war finance did not create the difficulties for the Bank of Ireland that they had for the Bank of England. A part of the Irish government deficit was covered by borrowing in England, and there were large imports of gold and silver into Ireland in the years 1795 to 1797, both on private account and for the Bank of Ireland.[1] No figures are available as to the specie reserve of the Bank of Ireland in the years before 1797, at the time of the suspension of payments,[2] or at any time during the Restriction. There was some internal drain of gold in Ireland in February, 1797,[3] but it appears to have been far less severe than in England.

In view of the dependence of the Bank of Ireland upon the Bank of England as a source of gold in time of crisis, there is serious question as to how long the Bank of Ireland could have continued specie payments had it not been able to obtain gold freely from the Bank of England. Not until 1821 did the Bank of Ireland open an account with the Bank of England, but even before 1797 it had, through its London agents, turned to the Bank of England as the final source of gold in time of crisis. Whatever the law or the directors of the Bank of Ireland might say, the economic realities were, in the words of the Lords Committee of Secrecy of 1797:

> "The Bank of England . . . is subject . . . to be called on for Cash, directly or indirectly, by those who are in Want of it, and is necessarily sensible of every material Failure or Distress, which arises from any Deficiency of Want of Coin, in every Part of this Kingdom or Ireland."[4]

[1] Report of 1804, Appendix U and W.

[2] In the hearings before the Committee of 1804 William Colville, a Director of the Bank of Ireland, in response to a question as to whether the Bank of Ireland would have had to suspend specie payments in the absence of Restriction, replied:

> "That is a very delicate question, and goes almost to the length of asking the quantity of Specie that existed in the Bank of Ireland at that period; and that being a subject upon which I have taken oath not to give any information upon, with great humility I hope that it will not be pressed further." P. 122.

The Secretary of the Bank of Ireland, in reply to my inquiry, wrote in 1952 that the Bank has no information on its specie holdings in the Restriction period.

[3] *Report of the Lords Committee of Secrecy*. 1797, pp. 262–263.

[4] *Op. cit.*, p. 250.

The Bank of England, whose reserve position had been seriously weakened in 1795 and 1796, largely as the result of loans and subsidies to Great Britain's continental allies, but partly because of the flow of specie to Ireland, faced an alarming internal run in February, 1797. Pitt secured an Order in Council, ordering the Bank to suspend specie payments when it opened for business on Monday morning, February 26. This Order was confirmed by the Bank Restriction Act of May 3, 1797,[1] which with its numerous extensions prolonged the suspension of specie payments until 1821. The Order in Council and the subsequent Restriction Act had applied only to the Bank of England, but the English country banks and the Scottish Banks, although making occasional payments in specie in the early years of the Restriction, were tacitly given the right to pay in Bank of England notes, thus in effect linking up the whole British currency system with the Bank of England note.[2]

The legal situation in Ireland, with its separate Parliament, was quite different. The Bank of Ireland as well as the private banks continued for nearly a week after the English suspension to make payments in specie, and there was no run that made necessary a suspension of payments at the moment. But the British Government for reasons of policy wished to extend the Restriction to Ireland and on March 2, 1797, the Lord Lieutenant of Ireland sent a message to the Irish House of Commons that:

> ". . . he had, by the advice of the privy council, issued an order to the governor and company of the bank of Ireland . . . similar to an order issued by the privy council of Great Britain, to the governor and company of the bank of England, directing them, for the present, to discontinue payments in specie."[3]

Both as a matter of economic policy and as a question of the prerogatives of the Irish Parliament the action of the Council aroused opposition. Henry Grattan, in line with a view that he had expressed many times before on other issues involving the authority of the Irish Parliament, criticized the Privy Council for issuing an order while the Irish Parliament was in session without first submitting the matter to the Parliament.[4] In the debate in the Commons, Thomas Pelham stated that:

> "The measure had been adopted here; not through any sort of inability on the part of the bank to answer its engagements, for the

[1] 37 G. III, c. 45.

[2] The legal status of the issues of the British and Irish banks in this period is covered in my article, "Legal Tender During the English and Irish Bank Restrictions," *Journal of Political Economy*, Vol. LVIII, No. 3, June, 1950, pp. 241–253.

[3] *The Parliamentary Register or History of the Proceedings and Debates of the House of Commons of Ireland.* Vol. XVII (Dublin, 1801, p. 404).

[4] *Ibid.*, March 15, 1797, p. 452.

> measure was not adopted at the desire of the bank directors; on the contrary, it was against their wishes; but it was pressed on them by government, as a necessary measure, in consequence of a similar one adopted in England."[1]

But on April 20, 1797, the Irish Commons voted "that it is the opinion of this House, that it is necessary to confirm and continue the measures taken by the bank of Ireland,"[2] and after approval by the Lords, the Irish Restriction became law on July 3, 1797.[3]

The Irish Restriction Act did not apply to banks other than the Bank of Ireland, but in line with the situation in England all Irish Banks in practice were relieved of the obligation to pay in specie. However some Irish banks continued for a time to make payments in specie,[4] and one leading Dublin bank, apparently in protest against the Restriction, redeemed all of its outstanding notes in gold and issued no more notes during the Restriction.[5]

After the Act of Union the Irish Restriction was assimilated to the English Restriction, but with the difference that the Bank of Ireland was permitted to follow an independent monetary policy, something which by the prevailing practice throughout the Restriction Period of requiring the English country banks and Scottish banks to meet their obligations in Bank of England funds, had been denied to those banks. It was this development that led to the special problem of Irish exchange in the Restriction Period.

MONETARY AND BANKING SITUATION RESULTING FROM THE RESTRICTION

The suspension of specie payments in England and Ireland created a new monetary situation, with a series of most interesting theoretical issues and practical problems. The notes of the Bank of Ireland became a free currency, independent not only of the precious metals but also of

[1] *Ibid.*, March 6, 1797, p. 405. [2] *Ibid.*, p. 485. [3] 37 G. III, c. 51.

[4] Sir Laurence Parsons stated in the Irish House of Commons, nearly two weeks after the original order of the Lord Lieutenant, that two banks in Dublin were still paying in specie. *The Parliamentary Register*, March 15, 1797, p. 453.

[5] Testimony of Peter La Touche before the Lords *Select Committee on The Circulation of Promissory Notes in Scotland and Ireland.* 1826. Pp. 96, 98.

> ". . . since the Restriction in the Year 1797 we have never issued a Note payable to Bearer. . . . I was not a partner in the House when the Restriction took place; but my Father, who was at the Head of the Establishment has often declared his Opinion to me, that a Banker never should issue a Note to Bearer that he did not pay in Gold; and as soon as the Restriction took place in England, and consequently in Ireland, the House from that Period never issued a Note to Bearer, and those Notes that were out they always paid in Gold."

the paper currency of England. The situation was similar to that which would have existed in the United States in 1933 if, simultaneously with the suspension of gold payments, one of the smaller Federal Reserve Banks had ceased to convert its deposits and notes at par into New York funds. The special situation in Northern Ireland complicated matters still further. In southern Ireland, where much business was already carried on in Bank of Ireland notes or in notes redeemable in Bank of Ireland notes, the suspension of specie payments, especially as the notes did not for some time go to an appreciable discount in gold,[1] meant a shift to the new free standard with little disturbance, and probably unnoticed by most of the population. In Northern Ireland, where bank notes were virtually unknown, business continued to be carried on in gold coin. Northern and southern Ireland gradually shifted to separate monetary standards, without anyone having planned it that way, and apparently with few persons at the time understanding the real significance of the development.

A further problem arising out of the simultaneous breaking of the link of the Irish currency with gold and with English currency was the disappearance from circulation of much of the existing silver coin, and the encouragement that this gave to the issue of bank notes of small denominations. The condition of the silver coinage in Ireland probably would have gotten steadily worse even had there been no Restriction. Coins near legal weight were going to the melting pot, and there had been a deterioriation in the weight and appearance of the coins still in circulation.[2] As long, however, as the English and Irish monetary systems were linked together on a gold basis at a fixed ratio of 13 to 12, there were some limits to the disorder in the silver currency of Ireland. English coins passed current in Ireland at the official rate of 13 pence Irish for 12 pence English, and before 1797 there was no more tendency for Ireland than for England to lose silver coins by melting or export. After the Restriction Act the circulation of silver coinage in Ireland was placed in danger by two developments: the depreciation of English currency in terms of Hamburg exchange, and the depreciation of Bank of Ireland notes in terms of English currency. As Hamburg was on the silver

[1] The figures for the premium on guineas in Dublin, published by the Committee of 1804, Appendix L, begin only in 1799. In January and February of that year the premium was $\frac{3}{4}$ of 1 per cent. Robert Marshall, in testimony before the Committee of 1804, spoke of a premium of 6d. to 9d. [$2\frac{1}{2}$ per cent to $3\frac{3}{4}$ per cent] being paid for guineas in Dublin shortly after the Restriction, but said that specie shops first appeared in Dublin in April 1798, and that dealings in gold started on the Exchange in March 1799. P. 105.

[2] The situation of the British silver coins is treated in detail in Lord Liverpool's *A Treatise on the Coins of the Realm* (London, 1805), pp. 185–188. He points out that tests made in 1798 showed a greater deficiency below the legal weight than in 1783. In 1798 the shillings tested were 25 per cent, and the sixpences 38 per cent, below legal weight.

standard, any depreciation of English currency in terms of Hamburg exchange was closely associated with a rise in the London price of silver.

The first development—the depreciation of London exchange in terms of Hamburg exchange—would encourage the melting or exporting of silver coin and would create difficulties for both England and Ireland. The second development—the depreciation of Dublin exchange in terms of London exchange—would complicate matters still further for Ireland as it would mean (*a*) that silver coin in Ireland would go to the melting pot even sooner than silver coin in England, and (*b*) that English silver, even though not driven to the melting pot or exported, would no longer circulate in Ireland when the Irish-English exchange rate rose much above 8 1/3.

In view of the shortage of silver coin in England before 1797, any rise in the Dublin-London rate almost certainly fostered the shipment from Ireland to England of any coin that would pass current in England. This would have been true even though the Irish currency had maintained or improved its old relationship to silver and to the Hamburg exchange. On the other hand, had the Dublin-London rate remained at par, any depreciation of the English pound in terms of Hamburg exchange would have tended equally to drain silver from Ireland and Britain to the continent or to send it to the melting pot. As matters developed after 1798, and particularly after 1802, the Irish pound depreciated in relation both to the English pound and to silver, with the result that shortly after the turn of the century the coinage situation in Ireland became chaotic.

The shortage of small coin in turn reacted on the general monetary situation, in that it encouraged the widespread, and in many cases illegal, issue of small notes, which probably exceeded the silver that was withdrawn from circulation.[1] Shortly after the Restriction country bankers in Ireland, as well as private parties not registered as bankers, began to issue "silver notes,"[2] which were supposed to be redeemable in silver coin, but which all too frequently appear to have been inconvertible

[1] Lord Liverpool recognized this relation between the state of the silver coin and the issues of the country banks, in his remark that "especially in the southern parts of Ireland, small Notes have been issued to supply the place of Silver Coins, of which there is certainly a great deficiency." *Op. cit.*, p. 219.

[2] A witness in 1804, asked to estimate the silver coin circulating outside of Dublin, answered, "I cannot, on account of the circulation being carried on by Silver Notes almost exclusively throughout the country of Ireland, excepting the North." Thomas Thorpe Frank, p. 74. In 1801 Edward Cooke, Under Secretary of the Civil Department of Ireland, wrote to Viscount Castlereagh, Chief Secretary of the Civil Department, "I understand private banks are doing mischief, and aiding the speculations in keeping up corn, and that mischief is doing by issuing small notes for silver currency." *Memoirs and Correspondence of Viscount Castlereagh.* (London, 1849), Vol. IV, p. 79.

even in terms of the debased silver coin. Evidence of the situation is given by the testimony of Jeremiah D'Olier, a Director of the Bank of Ireland, before the Committee of 1804. D'Olier, in the tradition of caution and understatement that bankers sometimes show when examined by legislative committees, indicated that the notes had been a problem, at least for the people who received them.

> "Have any inconveniences of losses attended that species of circulation called Silver Notes?—I believe there have to the holders of those Notes?——
>
> Through what means?—By the inability of the persons who issued them to pay them."[1]

In addition, the practice became increasingly common of merchants issuing I.O.U.'s, which frequently were not payable in cash on demand, but at best were simply accepted in trade by the issuer. The situation was in part facilitated by Irish legislation of 1799,[2] which permitted country banks to issue notes of less than £1, providing they were payable on demand in Bank of Ireland notes. Information supplied to the Committee of 1804 indicates that issues were made on a wholesale scale by many concerns that were not registered as bankers. Of 225 issuers of "Bank Notes, Silver Notes, and I.O.U.'s," 25 were shown as issuing Gold and Silver Notes, 62 as issuing Silver Notes, and 128 as issuing I.O.U.'s, in addition to six bankers in "Dublin City" and one in Waterford who apparently issued only regular notes.[3]

Letters in 1799 and 1801 to Viscount Castlereagh, then Chief Secretary of the Civil Department for Ireland, have revealing comments on the banking situation as seen by officials in Dublin. On March 21, 1799, George Rose, Secretary to the Treasury, wrote:

> "It may have happened that bankers and others may have lately issued more notes than usual, from the necessity of keeping gold to answer them being lessened, from the general understanding that no man's credit can be hurt by his not being able to pay in cash."[4]

About the same time Edward Cooke wrote to Castlereagh:

"The private bankers make Bank of Ireland Notes their capital, by

[1] P. 77.   [2] 39 G. III, c. 48.

[3] Appendix N. In addition, in Kinsale "several Shopkeepers" and in Cork "every Shopkeeper and Publican" issued I.O.U.'s.

In the district of Youghall of 70 note issuers, only one was a registered banker, seven issued silver notes, and 62 issued I.O.U.'s. The occupation of the issuers included among others: Shopkeeper, Baker, Grocer, Chandler, Wool Comber, Spirit Retailer, Strong Water Retailer, Maltster, Brewer, Tobacco Manufacturer, Innkeeper, Miller, and Tanner.

[4] *Memoirs and Correspondence of Viscount Castlereagh.* (London, 1848.) Vol. II, p. 219.

which means nine paper capitals may be issued for one in cash, which leads to general bankruptcy; or, if the Bank, aware of the practice of the bankers, do not issue their usual quantity of paper, it follows that the National Bank is crippled, and that their capital is used to their ruin."[1]

The result of these developments, together with the increase of the Bank of Ireland's circulation by 1802 to four times what it had been in 1797, was a substantial, but undetermined, expansion in the monetary circulation of Ireland in the years immediately following the suspension of cash payments.[2]

EXCHANGE RATES UNDER THE RESTRICTION

The first three years of the Restriction had little effect on exchange rates in either Ireland or England. The London-Hamburg exchange, and the London price of gold, showed only minor fluctuations. Until January, 1799, fluctuations in the Dublin-London rate were no greater than they had been for several years previous to the Restriction, and part of the time the Irish pound was at a small premium as compared with the British pound.[3] The Irish pound, with minor exceptions, behaved as though it were on a sterling exchange standard. It is not likely that such a relationship would have continued for more than two years had there not been some conscious policy on the part of the Bank of Ireland, or of the British or Irish Government, of holding a stable rate. There is no direct evidence that the Bank of Ireland had any such policy, and the testimony of its Directors in 1804, thoroughly dominated by the idea that exchange rates are independent of monetary policy, was all to the effect that the Bank of Ireland not only made no effort to maintain a stable Dublin-London rate, but that it was beyond its power to do so.[4] It appears, however, to have been the practice of the British Government

[1] *Ibid.*, Vol. II, p. 294. The letter is not dated but is endorsed "April, 1799."

[2] See below, pp. 33-40, for a more detailed analysis of the monetary expansion of the period, and of its relation to Bank of Ireland policy.

[3] See Chart 1.

[4] In the Restriction period, as had been the practice previously, Irish exchange in London was customarily quoted in terms of 21 day sight bills on Dublin, and London exchange in Dublin was customarily quoted in terms of 21 day sight bills on London. This meant that ordinarily the Dublin rate was higher than the London rate by a figure representing interest for a little less than two months. A comparison of the London and Dublin rates from 1794 to March, 1810, shows that at every date the London rate was above the Dublin rate, and that the difference averaged over one point. John Puget, the London agent of the Bank of Ireland, testified in 1804 that the difference between London-Dublin and the Dublin-London rate "in general is from 1 to 1½."

In the light of all the evidence it is reasonable to consider a London rate of 109 to 109½ as representing the par of exchange for the customary method of quoting exchange.

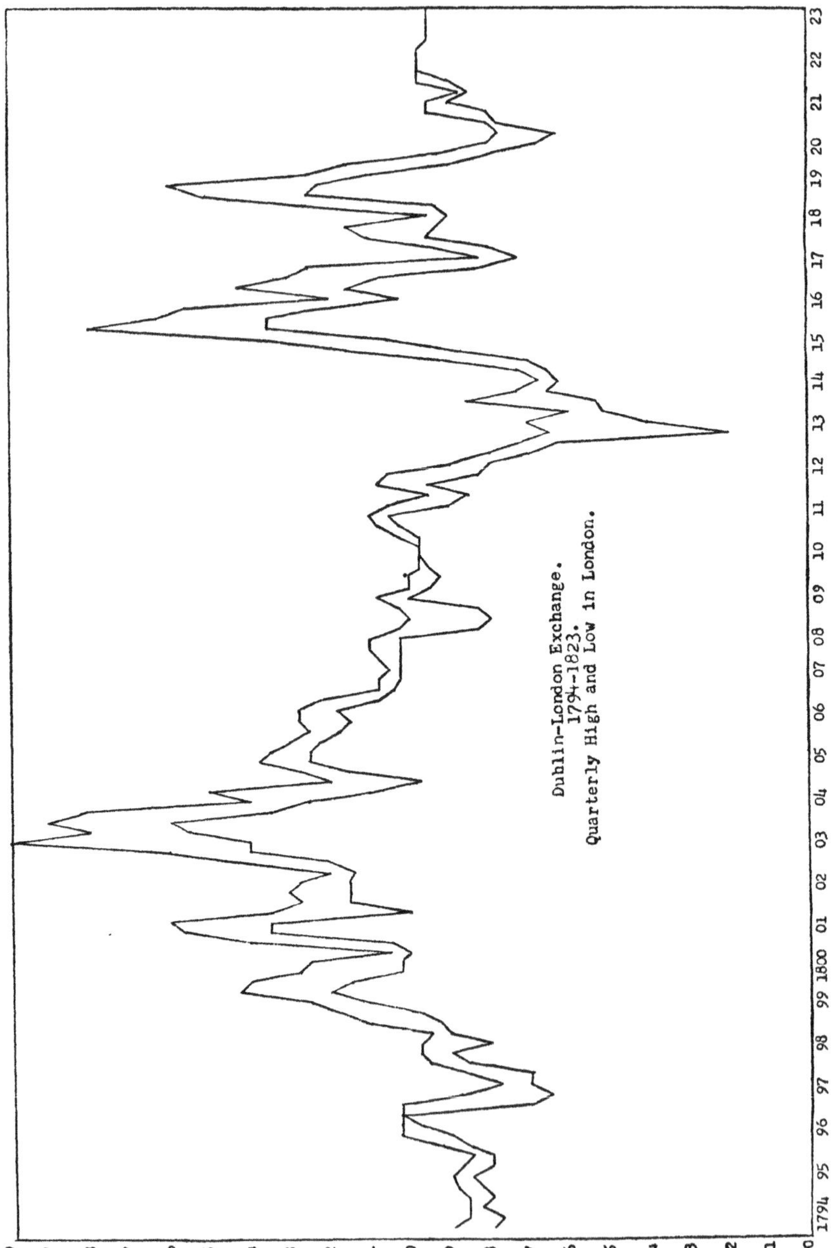
Dublin-London Exchange.
1794-1823.
Quarterly High and Low in London.

CHART 1.

from time to time to hold a stable Dublin-London rate during Irish loan operations, although it had no consistent or long sustained policy in the matter.

In 1798, at the time of the revolt of the United Irishmen, a loan of £1,500,000 raised in England was transmitted to Ireland in Bank of England notes, and according to the testimony of a witness before the Committee of 1804 the transfers:

> "... were negotiated at various rates of Exchange, not exceeding 6 per cent; by which means the Paper of the Bank of Ireland was kept on a par with Specie at the time the Rebellion was at its greatest height, and close to Dublin; . . ."[1]

Again in 1800, when another Irish loan was raised in England, the British Government fixed the rate for a time. According to the testimony in 1804 of John Puget, the London agent for the Bank of Ireland, who handled a large part of the loan transfers, the practice of the Irish Treasury just before 1800 in transferring funds from London to Dublin, was either to buy in London bills on Dublin at the market rate, or to have the Lords of the Treasury of Ireland draw on Puget's house.[2] Early in 1800 the exchange rate in London was around 14. At the instance of a group of merchants, and apparently without any clearly defined objectives, the British Government proceeded to buy Bank of Ireland notes in London at a rate of 9½. Walter Borrowes, a London merchant, described this operation in his testimony before the Irish Currency Committee of 1804:

> "It was in 1799 there was a tendency of the Exchange to rise equivalent to the depreciation of the Bank of Ireland Notes, which induced the merchants in the Irish trade in London to meet, and afterwards to wait on the Chancellor of the Exchequer (Mr. Pitt) to represent to him the difficulties which were growing in the commercial intercourse between Great Britain and Ireland in consequence of the high Exchange, and to entreat that some measure should be adopted to lessen it, if not remove it altogether. Mr. Pitt in consequence agreed that an instalment on the Loan then depending, which had been raised in Great Britain for the service of Ireland should be received at the Bank of

[1] Walter Borrowes, p. 25. If Borrowes' statement is correct, the transfers at this rate must have been made outside the market, as in 1798 the lowest Dublin quotation was 7⅜, and the lowest London quotation was 8½. Presumably the "rates of Exchange, not exceeding 6 per cent" were granted only to a favoured group of merchants, as was the case with loan transfers in 1800 and 1801.

[2] Pp. 19–22.

England in Bank of Ireland Notes, at the Exchange of 9½ per cent. which had the effect of lowering the then Exchange very considerably and proportionably, taking off the depreciation on the Bank Notes of Ireland, and the Exchange at Dublin was immediately reduced to that rate, or nearly so; and all the remittances out of Ireland, whether for payment of imports, or of rents to Absentees, or for remittances to the Bank of England, passed over at this Exchange, and continued to do so, so long as the Exchange of Bank of Ireland Notes continued at the Bank of England; and this principle was supported throughout the whole of the Loans of that Administration, and even a Loan for the service of Ireland, taken by an Irish house here in that Administration (1800) was taken in at the Bank of England at the same rate of Exchange, to the extent of about £200,000, and that about £900,000 was passed at the same rate in Dublin, under an expectation that when the interest of that Loan came to be remitted back, Government would take care that it should be done on equal terms of Exchange. In the next Administration (1801) similar applications were made to Mr. Addington to take in his Loans for Ireland at the Bank of England at the same rate of Exchange, which were refused, as the profits of Exchange were thought deserving the attention of Government: and since that time no assistance has been afforded to the Currency of Ireland, or to the rate of Exchange, by the transmission of Loans, more than their intrinsic weight carried with them."[1]

Despite Borrowes' statement that the Government's policy held the rate for Bank of Ireland notes at 9½ during the greater part of 1800, the publicly quoted market rate was so much above 9½ that it would appear that a few favoured persons were the principal beneficiaries of the low rate. The average rate in London for the year was 11⅜ and at no time in 1800 did the quotation go below 10. The average rate in Dublin was 10⅜, although for some months in the latter part of the year the rate was below 10. The suspicion that the operation was carried through without any larger monetary objectives in mind, and that its principal result was to benefit a few merchants at the expense of the Irish Treasury, is supported by the evidence of John Puget in 1804, who said that in 1800:

". . . at the instance of some merchants in England the Government was induced, with a view to lower the exchange, which was then 13¾,

[1] P. 29. William Coningham, also a London merchant, gave substantially the same account in his testimony before the Committee. Pp. 57–58.

Borrowes' testimony does not make clear when the 9½ rate was set, but the Table of the Dublin-London rates in London, in Appendix A2 of the 1804 Report, has a note for January, 1800, "Irish Bank Notes exchanged at the Bank of England this Year, at 9½ per Cent."

to 14 per cent, to exchange Bank of Ireland notes at 9½ per cent, for such parts of the Instalment of the Loan as became due to Ireland that year; . . . from examining the Account, though the foregoing method lowered the Exchange for the moment, it was found to be very partial in its operation, inasmuch as out of the £1,190,000 exchanged at the Bank, two houses alone got £409,000; and with five other houses got £687,000 so exchanged. . . . [The operation] fixed an Exchange lower than the rate at many times during that year; and it created much speculation on the Exchange, which was on the 30th Dec. 1800, 10½ per cent; on January 17th, 1801, 14 per cent; on the 31st Jan. 1801, 12½ per cent, a speculation arising from the uncertainty of these payments continuing, besides that the mode adopted, as to some of the payments almost precluded any but merchants, or those connected with them, deriving any benefit from the measure, for the Bank of England did not directly exchange Irish Bank Notes for English Bank Notes, but gave a preference to those who brought in Irish paper as a proportion of their payments on the English Loan; . . ."[1]

Puget's testimony further shows that in 1800 this special rate of 9½ was fixed only while loan instalments were being transferred, and that sometimes the instalments would be disposed of in three days, after which the rate apparently was left to fluctuate without any control by the Treasury.

The relatively small fluctuations in the London-Dublin rate[2] in the first six years of the Restriction seemed to have aroused little popular interest. One evidence of this is that virtually nothing appeared in print before 1803 on the Irish exchange situation, in contrast to the outpouring of pamphlet literature on the subject in 1803, 1804, and 1805. Any public interest that there might have been in the Irish exchange rates in 1799 and 1800 was overshadowed by the discussion in those years of the Union between Great Britain and Ireland. Government officials, however, were concerned about the monetary and exchange situation in Ireland, and discussed privately the possibility of action even before public debate broke out. Lord King, writing in 1803, spoke of the earlier concern of Irish officials over the policy of the Bank of Ireland.[3] This statement is confirmed by private correspondence, which shows that high government officials were considering measures to stabilize the exchange rate between Dublin and London, and even to consolidate the note issues of

[1] P. 22.

[2] After the Restriction the Dublin rate in London did not reach 10 until 1799, and except in the period from October, 1799, to January, 1800, it did not reach 13 until January, 1801.

[3] *Thoughts on the Effects of the Bank Restrictions*, pp. 79–80.

the Bank of England and the Bank of Ireland.[1] Apparently, however, these discussions did not lead to any action by Government, or to any public controversy.

PUBLIC CONTROVERSY ON THE IRISH EXCHANGE

General public discussion of the effects of the English Restriction on the monetary and exchange situation started early in 1801, when Walter Boyd published his *Letter to William Pitt . . . on the Influence of the Stoppage of Issues in Specie at the Bank of England.* In uncompromising terms he blamed the expansion in the note issues of the Bank of England for the rising commodity prices, the gold premium, and the depreciation of the English currency in terms of Hamburg exchange. This was followed shortly by a number of rejoinders defending the Bank, of which Sir Francis Baring's *Observations on the Publications of Walter Boyd, Esq., M.P.* (1801) was the most important. In 1802 Henry Thornton published his classic on *The Paper Credit of Great Britain*, and in a much more judicious way than Boyd criticized the Bank of England for its inflationary policy. At the same time the various bills for extending the English Restriction produced in 1800 and 1801 a revival of Parliamentary oratory on the monetary situation and on the foreign exchanges. Previous to May, 1803, there was no discussion of the Irish exchange situation in the British Parliamentary debates. Except for a discussion in 1802 in Jasper Atkinson's *Considerations on the propriety of the Bank of England resuming its payments in specie*, only incidental reference was made to the Irish situation in pamphlet literature previous to 1803, and Thornton made no mention of it in his book.

In 1802, following the Peace of Amiens, the Hamburg price of London exchange rose, and this improvement in the English paper pound continued well into 1805. In January, 1803, the Irish pound, already at a small discount in relation to London, depreciated further in relation to the English pound, and until October of that year its position got steadily

[1] On January 14, 1800, Edward Cooke wrote in detail to John Beresford, a member of the Privy Council, about the advantages and disadvantages of a fluctuating rate, but on balance strongly opposed stabilization principally on the ground that depreciation encouraged exports, discouraged imports and imposed a tax on absentee landlords. In conclusion he stated: "I trust, therefore, Mr. Pitt will not be induced to interfere." *The Correspondence of Right Hon. John Beresford*, . . . (London, 1854). Vol. II, p. 239.

Walter Borrowes, a London merchant who testified before the Committee of 1804, wrote to Beresford on July 10, 1801, of a conference with Henry Addington, the British Prime Minister, in which he told Addington: ". . . what we wanted was a common medium of paper to be substituted in room of the specie locked up by order of the Government," and reported that Addington was greatly interested in clearing up the exchange, and ". . . he [Addington] thought the consolidation of the Banks the most likely to accomplish this purpose." *Ibid.*, Vol. II, pp. 255.

worse. In January, 1803, the London quotation was 12; in March it reached 14¾, in August, 18½, and in September it went to 20.

General public discussion of the Irish exchange situation started early in 1803, and undoubtedly was prompted by the increasing premium on London exchange. However, the improvement of the English currency in relation to Hamburg probably would have made the public more conscious of the Irish monetary and exchange problems even had there been no further depreciation of the Irish currency in relation to London. As it was, the depreciation of Dublin exchange, at a time when London exchange was strengthening in relation to Hamburg, and criticism of the Bank of England on account of the Hamburg exchange situation had virtually ceased, explains why, both as an economic issue and as a political issue, the Irish situation should have come to the fore in 1803. To the public, or to members of Parliament, who were critical of the British Government or of banks, a depreciation of the English pound in relation to Hamburg, or a depreciation of the Irish pound in relation to London, provided equally good opportunities for attacking the Government's policies or the behaviour of bankers.

Parliamentary discussion of the Irish exchange started with Lord King's speech of May 3, 1803, on the bill to continue the Irish restriction until three months after the resumption of payments by the Bank of England.[1] King attributed the state of the Irish exchange to the excessive note issues in Ireland, and moved an amendment that the Bank of Ireland be required to redeem its notes in Bank of England notes. The amendment was defeated.[2] Shortly thereafter King expanded his argument into a booklet, *Thoughts on the Effects of the Bank Restrictions*, and this was followed by a second and expanded edition in 1804. The large number of pamphlets on the Irish exchange that appeared shortly in both England and in Ireland show the great popular interest in the subject at that time.[3]

APPOINTMENT OF THE PARLIAMENTARY COMMITTEE OF 1804

Shortly after Parliament reopened in November, 1803, the situation of the Irish currency was debated at length in both the Commons and

[1] *Parliamentary History*, Vol. XXXVI, p. 1247.

[2] *Ibid.*, May 5, 1803, p. 1248.

[3] In the Library of the Royal Irish Academy in Dublin are a number of pamphlets on the Irish monetary and exchange situation, mostly published between 1803 and 1805, which are not in the Goldsmiths' Library at the University of London, the Seligman Library at Columbia University, or the Kress Collection at Harvard University. Most of them are of no doctrinal importance, but are of significance as showing the great current interest in the problem. A list of the publications of the period on Irish money banking, and exchange is given in Appendix 1.

the Lords. After considerable legislative jockeying, John Foster, the Secretary of State for Ireland, who had been the last Speaker of the Irish Parliament before the Union, moved on March 2, 1804, for the appointment of a committee to investigate the condition of the Irish Currency. The motion was carried, Foster was made chairman, and three days later the committee opened its hearings.

The circumstances surrounding the appointment of this Committee, and the subsequent Parliamentary treatment of its Report, raise issues which relate more directly to the nature of public opinion, and to the functioning of legislative bodies, than to economic analysis in the narrower sense. Yet I believe that for the economist who is interested in economic issues in their larger setting it is worth while to examine in detail the political background of the Irish committee because we can see in this case the political and personal forces back of a debate that economists, looking at the more obvious evidence in the form of Committee hearings and reports, are likely to treat as primarily an analysis of a technical economic problem.

As suggested earlier, monetary transactions, and particularly foreign exchange operations, at this period affected directly the economic fortunes of only a small part of the population of Ireland. In comparison with the current political disorders in Ireland, and with the economic problems arising out of the trade disturbances of the Napoleonic Wars and out of the Restriction by the Bank of England, the effect on Irish life of a fluctuation of 10 per cent in the exchange rate on London was a minor problem. In so far as high prices were a problem in Ireland,[1] the depreciation in the Irish pound in terms of the British pound was a relatively unimportant factor. For only two groups, the absentee landlords and merchants dealing between England and Ireland, would the Dublin-London exchange fluctuations appear as a major problem in an economic picture badly disturbed from so many other sources. A depreciation of the Irish pound in terms of the British pound meant fewer

[1] No index number is available for Irish prices in the Restriction period, but there is a presumption that price movements in these years did not differ greatly from the movement of British prices, as shown by Silberling's index for the period, (Norman J. Silberling, "British Prices and Business Cycles, 1779–1850," *Review of Economic Statistics*, Preliminary Vol. V, Supplement 2, October, 1923, pp. 232–235) with slightly greater fluctuations in Irish than in British prices, due to the fluctuations in the Dublin-London rate.

Silberling's index of the annual average of the cost of living in England for the years since the suspension of payments (1790–100) is:

1797	120	1801	174
1798	121	1802	138
1799	143	1803	140
1800	170	1804	140

His index of commodity price rises in 1803, with the average for the last three quarters about 10 per cent higher than in 1802.

British pounds from a given rent paid in Irish bank paper,[1] although as pointed out later,[2] there is serious doubt whether the absentee landlord was in any worse position on this account than was the landlord who resided in Ireland and spent his rents for local products and services or imported goods.

The initial criticism in the House of Commons of the Irish monetary and exchange situation came from Lord Archibald Hamilton, who in a debate on December 6, 1803, on a bill to extend the Restriction by the Bank of Ireland, had announced that he intended to move "that there should be a restriction of paper circulation in Ireland."[3] He did not press the matter, however, but over two months later, he referred to his proposed motion and stated in cryptic terms:

> "He had made it his business to inquire into the subject with the greatest care, and he had endeavoured to ascertain the sentiments of persons the best informed on matters connected with the situation of Ireland; and the result of his inquiries had been a conviction that it would, for the present, be expedient not to press the motion."[4]

Following Hamilton's statement that he would not make a motion, an extended debate took place in which ten members participated. Lord Henry Petty spoke of the seriousness of the Irish monetary situation, and said that "he was most clearly of opinion that some strong measure ought without delay to be adopted";[5] John Foster said that "it undoubtedly was the duty of Parliament to enter, as soon as possible, into an investigation of the state of the circulation in Ireland."[6] Henry Thornton, in a careful review of the Irish situation, stated his belief "that the bad state of exchange in Ireland, arose from the too great circulation of paper," and indicated that he would like to have Parliament make an investigation.[7]

A week later Lord Archibald Hamilton, who two months earlier had initiated the discussion of the Irish monetary situation, opened the debate on the Irish Bank Restriction Bill and referred to a situation which probably was an important factor in leading to the appointment of a Parliamentary Committee. He spoke of "another circumstance which he had heard," that the Lords of the Irish Treasury, whose salaries evidently were fixed in Irish pounds, were being paid in English pounds at the

[1] Landlords with properties in Northern Ireland until 1812 generally received their rents in gold at par. Hence, whether residents or absentees, they were not affected by the depreciation of the Irish paper pound. The details of this situation are discussed in pp. 248–250 of my article on "Legal Tender During the English and Irish Bank Restrictions."

[2] Pp. 46–47.

[3] Hansard, First Series, Vol. I, p. 1653.

[4] *Ibid.*, p. 1082. Feb. 13, 1804.

[5] *Ibid.*, p. 1088.

[6] *Ibid.*, p. 1089.

[7] *Ibid.*, p. 1090.

par of exchange. He "lamented" that he could not move for the appointment of a committee to investigate the Irish exchange, in view of his obligation to participate in another Parliamentary Committee, but he hoped that a committee would be moved for by Mr. Foster, "whose abilities and experience eminently qualified him for the task."[1]

Hamilton's accusation that Government officials were having payments due to them in Irish currency converted into English currency at par put the debate on a new basis. It made the Irish exchange problem not only an issue of economic policy, but also a question of misuse of public funds by government officials. Isaac Corry, the Chancellor of the Irish Exchequer, admitted that Hamilton's charges were true, but defended the practice as one that had originated with the Union and had been in effect since then.[2]

Even in the formal language of Hansard one can sense a bitterness in the exchanges between Hamilton and Corry, which continued a few days later when Hamilton moved that there be presented to the House an account of payments at par to government officials.[3] Two accounts laid before the House showed that a total of £38,721–18–6½. British money had been paid at par since the Union.[4] For many members the revelations must have turned a technical problem of monetary policy and foreign exchange into an issue that opposition members in a legislative body have always understood, no matter what the country or the age.

On March 2, 1804, Foster moved:

> "That a Committee be appointed to inquire into the causes of the present high rate of exchange between Great Britain and Ireland, and the state of the currency in the latter kingdom; and to report the same to the House."[5]

and after extended debate the motion was approved.[6]

The formal Parliamentary records between Hamilton's original statement on December 6, 1803, that he intended to move for a restriction of Irish bank paper and the approval, nearly three months later, of Foster's motion for a Committee suggest political manœuvering and behind-the-scenes negotiations, the exact nature of which can only be surmised. The record strongly suggests that Hamilton and Petty were the real forces back of the movement for a Parliamentary investigation. They also indicate that John Foster, who neither before nor after ever showed any great concern about problems of money and foreign exchange, had acted reluctantly and only after Government spokesmen had refused to take

[1] *Ibid.*, pp. 1101–1102, February 20, 1804.
[2] *Ibid.*, pp. 1102–1103.
[3] *Ibid.*, March 2, 1804, pp. 647–648.
[4] *Ibid.*, pp. 1163–1167.
[5] *Ibid.*, pp. 653.
[6] *Ibid.*, pp. 662.

any action.[1] The implication in several statements in Parliament that Isaac Corry and other government spokesmen, although they refused to initiate any action in regard to the Irish exchange situation, would not oppose such a motion if made by John Foster, is supported by a letter from London written by Edward Cooke to John Beresford on February 22:

> "I hear, Ministry are fools enough to have consented for Foster to move for a Committee into the state of the Irish Exchange and Paper Currency . . . Corry got quizzed for paying his own salary in specie, and is very sore. I think it was fair enough and he should laugh at the attack."[2]

The impression of the Parliamentary record as to Foster's role is supported by an unpublished letter of Francis Horner, later the prime mover and Chairman of the Bullion Committee,[3] to James Murray on February 17, 1804:

> "I think he [Petty] was not a little timid on the conclusion he came to about the Irish Bank, and I have told him so. Old Foster had been talking him over. And Foster, it appears to me, is not yet sufficiently familiarized with these subjects to see them in their real simplicity, or to hold them quite firmly enough. There never was so plain a case as this conduct of the Irish Bank."

Francis Horner's unpublished letter to his brother Leonard, undated but evidently written in April, 1804, when Leonard Horner was planning a trip to Ireland, is also illuminating, not only for its comments on the roles of Foster, Hamilton, and Petty, and its statement on the activity

[1] Foster on February 13 (*Ibid.*, 1089) had expressed the hope that the "subject would be taken up, particularly by some gentlemen on the treasury bench." On February 20 he said, in response to Lord Hamilton's suggestion that he move for the appointment of a committee, that: "He was sorry he could not undertake . . . to move for a committee to inquire into this subject," but hoped that the gentlemen on the Treasury Bench would (pp. 1105). The same day he reiterated his hope that the Ministers would take up the subject, "but as they remained silent, he felt the call upon him so imperiously, that he would, on a future date, bring the matter under the consideration of Parliament, . . ." (pp. 1105). On February 24 he repeated his hope that "some motion . . . would have been made from a quarter that was best capable of giving it effect; but as he has been disappointed in that expectation, he would not hesitate any longer to take the business on himself" (pp. 1111).

[2] *The Correspondence of Right Hon. John Beresford,* Vol. II, pp. 272–273. Beresford's correspondents were not in agreement on the propriety of payment at the par of exchanges of officials whose salaries were fixed in Irish currency, as on April 6, 1804, Lord Auckland wrote to Beresford: "Who were the profligate fellows who robbed the Irish Exchequer in order to pay themselves the unfavourable exchanges?" P. 284.

[3] In 1938, through the courtesy of Lady Eleanor Langman, the grandniece of Francis Horner, I was able to consult the papers of Francis Horner. These contain many items on the monetary controversy of the Restriction period that do not appear in his published papers.

of Henry Thornton on the Committee, but also for its evidence as to the interest that Horner himself took in the appointment of the Committee, and as to his contact with and possibly his influence on the members of the Committee.

> "I have found in London the Dublin pamphlet I mentioned in my last, called an 'Inquiry into the Depreciation, etc.' so that you will be spared the trouble of getting it for me in Belfast . . . you would oblige me . . . if you would make yourself master of the subject of Irish exchange and currency, when you are on the spot, where particular inquiries can be made; not that I think your brethren the merchants are in general very skilful in the art of communicating their information. There are one or two points in this subject of Irish circulation, which puzzle me very much; and which I find puzzle some of my friends who are upon the Parliamentary Committee about it. The inquiries of this Committee will give us a good many curious facts. Thornton attends these constantly; and he understands these matters better than anybody else in London. Lord Archibald Hamilton told me an anecdote very creditable to Foster, who is chairman; when he came over at the beginning of spring, he knew only the facts and details of the business, and of course had very confident prejudices and errors—he has since studied it in the general view, and has come over entirely to the plain and liberal opinions which a general view gives and can alone give. It is a curious proof of the degree in which Adam Smith's speculations and others of the kind are studied by the young men in Parliament, beyond the attention that was paid to such topics by the politicians who were educated at an earlier period of the last century; that Mr. Foster should have formed his opinion almost under the guidance of Hamilton and Petty, and Lord Grenville corrected his under Lord King."

The Committee was an unwieldy group of forty-nine persons, but five constituted a quorum. In addition to John Foster, the Chairman, among its members were Henry Addington (Prime Minister and Chancellor of The Exchequer), Viscount Castlereagh, George Canning, Isaac Corry, Lord Archibald Hamilton, Lord Henry Petty, George Rose, R. B. Sheridan, Henry Thornton, Samuel Thornton, George Tierney, and Nicholas Vansittart.[1] Of the twenty-two members of the Bullion Committee six were members of the Committee of 1804.[2] The membership included

[1] Details on the membership of the Committee are given in Appendix 4.

[2] Charles Long, William Manning, R. B. Sheridan, Earl Temple, George Tierney, Henry Thornton. The figures would be twenty-three and seven if George Rose, who was on the Bullion Committee for only two days and was replaced by Davies Giddy, were considered as a member of the Bullion Committee.

practically everyone, with the exception of Francis Horner and William Huskisson, who seven years later played a prominent role, either in support or in opposition, in the Parliamentary debates on the Bullion Report.

HEARINGS OF THE COMMITTEE

The hearings opened on March 5, 1804, and the committee went about its tasks in a business-like way. John Foster was in the chair throughout the hearings, but the centring of the questions around a few basic ideas, and the skilful cross-examination of the witnesses indicate careful planning of the hearings under the guidance of someone thoroughly familiar with the theory and practice of banking and foreign exchange. Both the testimony of Francis Horner as to Henry Thornton's activities on the Committee and the questions put to the witnesses suggest that Thornton had a major responsibility for the work of the Committee.[1] The main problem presented to the Irish Currency Committee was the same one that was presented to the Bullion Committee six years later: what are the causes of the fluctuations of exchange rates under inconvertible paper money? In 1804 the problem involved exchange between two countries, one of which—Great Britain—had an inconvertible paper money, the other of which—Ireland—had one area, the southern counties, in which inconvertible paper money was used, and another, Ulster, in which payments, including the purchase of London exchange, were customarily made in gold. There was no restriction on the movement of gold in any form between Ireland and England, or within Ireland, thus eliminating the problem of an illegal trade in gold that complicated so much of the Bullion Committee's discussion. Shipping costs between Ireland and England had not increased greatly since the suspension of cash payments, in contrast to the changes in the cost of shipment between England and the Continent. Furthermore, as a result of the Act of Union, the restrictions on trade between England and Ireland were less after 1800 than they had been in 1797, a situation quite different from that involved in the Bullion Committee's problem, where trade restrictions complicated the analysis of the effect of monetary expansion upon the exchanges. As in the hearings before the Bullion Committee, the question of remittances played a prominent role, but in the Irish case these remittances to absentee landlords had existed long before exchange fluctuations became a serious problem.

[1] The nature of many of the questions, and in some cases even their wording, is strikingly suggestive of the views that Thornton had expressed in his *Paper Credit of Great Britain*, and in his testimony before the Committees of Secrecy of Parliament in 1797. This is particularly true in the incisive questions on the "real bills" doctrine, and on the relation between the credit policy of the Bank of Ireland and the ability of other Irish banks to expand note issues.

The circumstances permitted the work of the Committee to be concentrated more on issues of theory and problems of policy than was possible with the Bullion Committee. The existence of an open premium on guineas in Ireland, of a publicly quoted exchange rate between Belfast and Dublin, and of a discount of Bank of Ireland notes in terms of Bank of England notes as measured by the exchange rate in both Dublin and London, reduced to a minimum the fruitless polemics over the existence of depreciation that took up so much time in the hearings before the Bullion Committee.

A large part of the queries put to the witnesses[1] were pointed to the following problems:

(1) What are the causes of exchange fluctuations?

(2) Is the private paper of Ireland dependent upon the volume of Bank of Ireland paper?

(3) Is it feasible for the Bank of Ireland to follow the policy of discounting all good paper?

(4) What policy would the Bank of Ireland need to follow in order to hold its notes at a parity with Bank of England notes?

CAUSES OF EXCHANGE FLUCTUATION

On the causes of the depreciation of the Irish paper and of appropriate banking policy under a suspension of payments, the spokesmen for the Bank of Ireland (Jeremiah D'Olier and William Colville, Ex-Governors and Directors) took the same position that the Bank of England authorities took six years later in their testimony before the Bullion Committee:

(*a*) Monetary policy had no effect upon the exchanges.

(*b*) Exchange fluctuations were due entirely to the balance of remittances[2] between Ireland and England.

(*c*) As long as the Bank of Ireland made its advances only upon sound security it was impossible to have an over-issue of notes.

The fact that Ireland and England were under the same sovereignty, that there were few limitations on Irish trade with England, that exchange

[1] A list of the witnesses is given in Appendix 5.

[2] The term "balance of remittances" or "balance of debt" was used in pamphlet literature of the period, in the hearings before the Committee, and in the Report of the Committee, without any clearcut definition. The context generally implies that the balance is the difference between the total of current account receipts and long term borrowing, and the total of current account payments and repayments on long term loans, thus making the balance equal in modern analysis to gold movements and short-term capital movements. There is, however, no discussion of short-term capital movements in the hearings of the Committee or in its Report, and the assumption seems always to be that the "balance" was payable in specie.

between Belfast, where payments in gold continued, and London was favourable to Belfast, and that exchange was not unfavourable to Scotland nor had it been unfavourable to Ireland previous to the Restriction, all made the official position a difficult one to defend. Yet these banking witnesses insisted that exchange rates were not influenced by banking policy, despite the admissions that they were forced to make under the skilful questioning of the chairman.

Colville maintained not only that the greatly increased issues of the Bank of Ireland had not depreciated the exchange, but insisted that by releasing gold for export the issues had improved the position of the Irish exchange.[1] D'Olier took an equally strong position. After expressing the view that when the balance of payments was in favour of Ireland the exchange would come back to par, he was asked: "Do you mean that this would equally be the case, whatever was the amount of the Paper circulation of Ireland?" and he replied, "I do."[2]

Other witnesses[3] agreed with this view that the situation of trade and other current payments explained the depreciation of the Irish currency, but Robert Marshall, the Inspector General of Imports and Exports of Ireland,[4] John Roach, a merchant of Dublin,[5] and William Coningham,[6] a merchant of London who later testified before the Bullion Committee, all believed that the expansion of note issues in Ireland was the principal cause for the adverse exchange. In less categorical terms, Thomas Thorpe Frank,[7] an exchange merchant of Dublin, and Robert Barnewall,[8] a merchant in London, supported the view that the monetary expansion in Ireland was responsible for the depreciation of the Irish exchange.

BANK OF IRELAND'S INFLUENCE ON THE MONETARY SUPPLY

It is clear that there had been a great expansion in the note circulation of the Bank of Ireland since 1797, proportionately much greater than that of the Bank of England,[9] but the meagre data on the note issues of

[1] Pp. 89–90, 97. See the extract from Colville's evidence on pp. 101–106.

[2] P. 118.

[3] In particular John Puget (p. 19) and Jeremiah Harman (pp. 36–40).

[4] Pp. 101–103. See the extracts from Marshall's evidence on pp. 111–117. The evidence of Marshall is of particular interest, as several hundred words are an exact quotation from two memoranda that he had prepared in February, 1804, previous to the appointment of the Committee. These memoranda are in the papers of the Earl of Hardwicke, then Lord Lieutenant of Ireland, in the British Museum. Add. Ms. 35, 746, ff. 273–281.

[5] Pp. 78–83. [6] Pp. 56–58. [7] Pp. 111–112.

[8] Pp. 49–51. Barnewall's evidence on this point is reprinted on pp. 96–98.

[9] The circulation of the Bank of England increased by about 80 per cent between February 28, 1797, and February 28, 1804; the circulation of the Bank of Ireland increased by over 300 per cent in approximately the same period. See Chart 2.

private banks, and the complications of forgeries, silver notes, I.O.U.'s, and counterfeit silver coin, make it impossible to form any accurate judgment as to the total monetary circulation of Ireland, or to state with assurance what control the Bank of Ireland, through its credit policy, exercised over other note issuing agencies.

Only on the circulation of Bank of Ireland notes were accurate figures available. On January 1, 1797, the circulation was £621,917; on April 1, 1797, it was £737,269. On January 1, 1804, the figure had reached £2,986,999, of which slightly over a £1,000,000 consisted of notes from £1 to 3 guineas, denominations which had not been issued prior to 1797. The new small denomination notes presumably replaced gold withdrawn from circulation, but in 1804 the circulation of notes of £5 and above, the only denominations in circulation at the time of the suspension of cash payments, was nearly three times what it had been seven years before. A part of this increase in the larger notes must also have been substituted for gold that circulated before the Restriction, but it would be pure guesswork to attempt an estimate.

As to the issues of private banks, there are no official figures, but estimates of three witnesses, who should have been as well informed on the matter as anyone in Ireland, indicated that in 1804 these were about £3,000,000, and that this was at least twice and perhaps three times the issue at the time of the suspension of cash payments in 1797.[1] A reasonable estimate would be that a note circulation of around £2,000,000 at the time of the suspension of payments in 1797 had increased in seven years to about £6,000,000, exclusive of I.O.U.'s.

A statement in one of the numerous pamphlets of the period, although on the dramatic side, would appear to be a fair summary of the monetary situation outside of Ulster and Dublin at the time of the Committee hearings:[2]

> "This *medium* in three provinces, (with exception of the metropolis) at this moment consists of a very moderate quantity of National Bank paper; a much larger amount of Dublin private Bank paper; an incal-

[1] John Roach, "on general surmise," estimated the issues, exclusive of those of the Bank of Ireland, as £3,000,000 "at least" (p. 82). William Colville, referring to the circulation of private bank notes, including the silver notes, said "to hazard a guess, for which I will not in any shape stand responsible, I should imagine it was equal to that of the Notes issued by the Bank of Ireland." (p. 86). John Claudius Beresford estimated the circulation of the private bankers of Dublin at "about £700,000," which he thought approximately the same as at the time of the Restriction. He was willing "to hazard a conjecture" that the circulation of country bank notes was "at least four times what it was," and although this estimate was supported by incomplete figures, his estimate would be consistent with a total country bank circulation in 1804 in the neighbourhood of £2,000,000 to £2,500,000. (Pp. 92–93).

[2] *A Candid Cobler's Cursory and Critical Conjectures on Exchange and Small-Change, on Balance of Trade, on Balance of Remittance, on Circulating Medium and Kite-Flying.* (1804) P. 7.

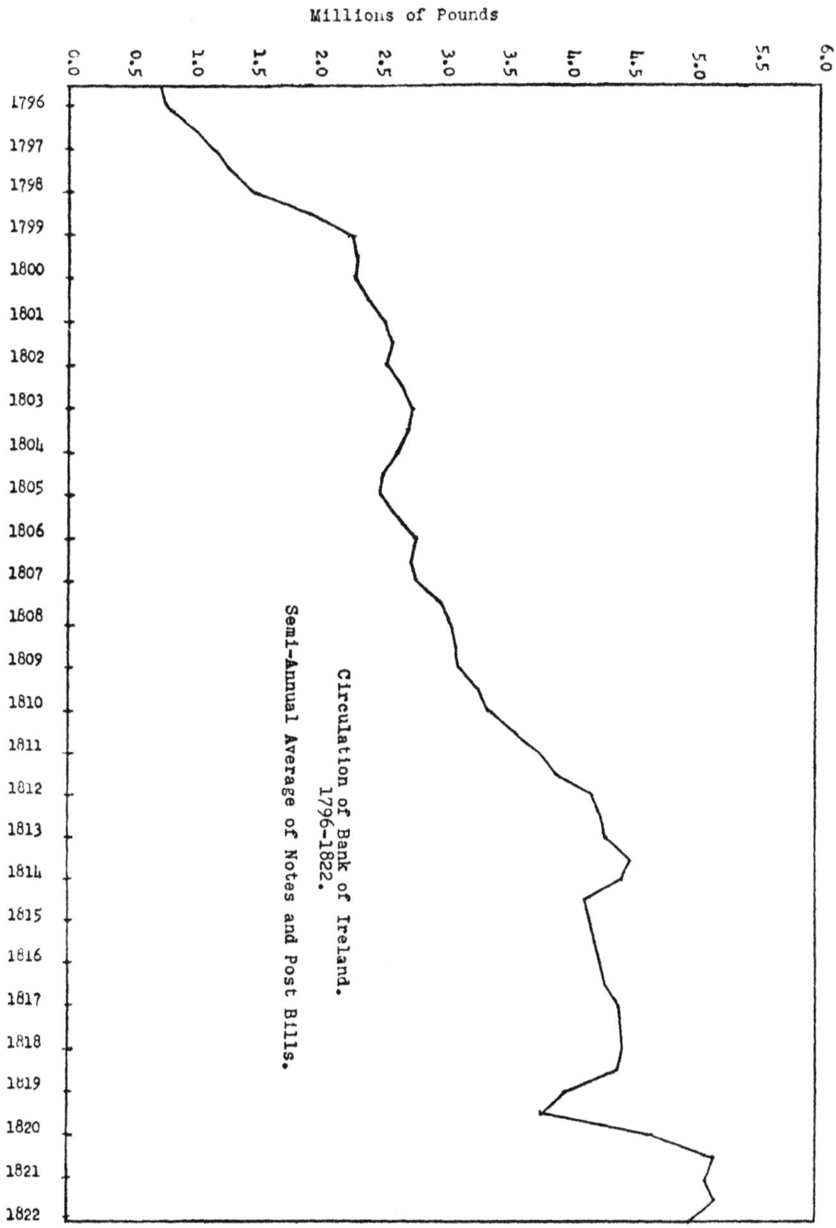
Millions of Pounds
Circulation of Bank of Ireland.
1796-1822.
Semi-Annual Average of Notes and Post Bills.

CHART 2.

culable influx of country coinage in paper, for gold and silver; and an accumulated mass of counterfeit silver and copper, base beyond sufferance, description or example."

After 1797, as before, notes of private Irish banks expressed in terms of pounds or guineas customarily were payable in Bank of Ireland notes. But despite this tie between the note issues of the private banks and the Bank of Ireland paper, it seems clear from the testimony of several witnesses that the total means of payment in southern Ireland did not bear a close proportional relationship to the Bank of Ireland note circulation. This loose relationship was the result of three situations: (1) the widespread issue of silver notes, which were promises to pay in silver coin, much of which was underweight, and in considerable part counterfeit; (2) the circulation of I.O.U.'s issued by unlicensed bankers, and in practice frequently redeemable only in the products sold by the issuer; and (3) the fact that the areas of circulation of Bank of Ireland notes and private notes were much less clearly divided than in England. To these might be added a fourth factor, the great number of counterfeit notes in circulation. The significance of the first two situations seems clear. The total of these notes would be only remotely connected with Bank of Ireland policy, except as the suspension of payments by the Bank of Ireland created a lax attitude on the part of others toward the honouring of their obligations, and a more tolerant public opinion toward such laxness.

The third situation presents a problem of great practical importance, involving some significant theoretical issues in central bank control. A bank, when its notes are used not only as a means of payment, but also as the reserves of other banks, is exercising a control over the total monetary supply, and is performing an essential central banking function.[1] Any discussion of the consequences of the expansion of credit by a central bank must consider both the nature of the existing relationship between the liabilities of the central bank and the liabilities of private banks, and also the significance that a change in this relationship may make in the effectiveness of a given credit policy of the central bank.

In the United States under the Federal Reserve System the division between private and central bank means of payment is not geographical, but is based entirely on the form of payment: all currency payments are in the form of central bank or treasury obligations, and all check payments by private parties are on private banks. Any shift in the proportion

[1] The hearings of the Committee of 1804, and other available evidence, indicate that deposit banking was of very limited importance in Ireland at this time. Hence, in my analysis of the effect of Bank of Ireland policy on the monetary situation I have ignored the possibility of check payments, or of the holding of bank reserves in the form of deposits with the Bank of Ireland.

of payments made by check might offset or might accentuate the effect of Federal Reserve policy. That is, an expansion of Federal Reserve credit might have no inflationary effect if accompanied by a shift from check to currency payments; and a deflationary policy might be more than offset by an increase in the proportion of payments made by check. In England around 1800 there was a differentiation, partly geographical, and partly functional, between the use of Bank of England and private bank obligations. In all of England outside of London, with the exception of Lancashire, practically all non-coin payments, whether by check or note, were in private bank obligations; in London all note payments and a substantial part of check payments were in Bank of England obligations. In addition, Bank of England notes served as reserves of country banks, and as reserves of private London banks, and the deposits in private London banks in turn served as reserves of country banks.

In the case of present-day American conditions, and of the English conditions outlined above, the effect of changes in central bank credit usually can be anticipated, because the geographic areas, and purposes of use, of private and central bank obligations are well defined, and the reserve practices of private banks ordinarily are not subject to rapid change. In Ireland, with the Bank of Ireland in operation for less than 15 years when the Restriction went into effect, the exact relationship between Bank of Ireland and private bank paper was so loosely defined, and apparently so subject to change, that the effect upon the total Irish means of payment of an increase or decrease in Bank of Ireland notes is much more difficult to determine.

The main problem, aside from that of private silver notes and I.O.U.'s not redeemable in Bank of Ireland paper, was the fact that there were no clearly defined areas of circulation of Bank of Ireland and private bank paper. In Dublin the Bank of Ireland notes and the notes of the Dublin bankers circulated side by side, and some Bank of Ireland notes were in circulation in practically all country districts of Ireland, outside of Ulster. Hence Bank of Ireland notes might serve as a means of payment, or as bank reserves, depending on the customs of the community. In every part of Ireland the private banks had the possibility of substituting their notes for Bank of Ireland notes. Such a development would, even in the absence of Bank of Ireland expansion, have permitted an expansion in total monetary supply, in the same way that in the United States today a shift from cash payments to check payments would permit an expansion of the means of payment.

There is no way of knowing to what extent there was such a shift from Bank of Ireland notes to private bank notes, but from the evidence it is clear that private bankers were making strenuous efforts to increase their circulation at the expense of Bank of Ireland notes. From the time of the establishment of the Bank of Ireland there had been competition between it and the private banks to expand their respective circulations. However, this rivalry seems to have been intensified after the suspension of payments in 1797, and two practices were a factor in extending the circulation of private paper. The army agents and yeomanry agents were required to make their payments in Bank of Ireland notes, but, presumably at a profit to themselves, frequently exchanged these notes for private bank paper and then made their payments in the private notes.[1] Furthermore, it was common practice for bankers, in order to increase the circulation of their notes, "to pay a commission to butter factors, corn-buyers, and other dealers, on the amount of paper they can issue."[2] Although no witnesses attempted to estimate the quantity of counterfeit notes in circulation, references in the literature of the period to counterfeits are common. The statement of Edward Wakefield, before the Bullion Committee, probably was equally true as a description of conditions in 1804

> "Under this head of Issues of Private Banks, I wish to add, that there is in Ireland a circulation of forged notes, of which no one here can form an idea, and the amount of which it is impossible to guess, although it is known to be enormous; indeed so large as to deserve a place in every calculation of the circulating medium of the sister island."[3]

The repeated questioning of witnesses on the relationship between Bank of Ireland circulation and the circulation of the private bankers showed an appreciation on the part of some member of the Committee of the reserve significance of central bank liabilities. The results of the cross-examination were inconclusive, partly because there was no clear-cut relation between Bank of Ireland paper and private bank paper, and partly because some of the witnesses were either unable or unwilling

[1] James Crofton, Evidence, p. 70; Walter Borrowes, Evidence, p. 25. Edward Wakefield in testimony in 1810 before the Bullion Committee (Folio edition) pp. 135–137, referred to the practice, although he stated that it was prohibited. *The Candid Cobler, op. cit.* also referred to the practice, p. 8. In 1802 Jasper Atkinson stated that a large part of army payments in Ireland were made by notes of a Dublin private banker. (*Considerations on the propriety of the Bank of England resuming its payments in specie.* Pp. 100–1). As early as 1799 Lord Viscount Donoughmore had denied in a speech in the Irish House of Lords that a Dublin bank was keeping up its note circulation by an arrangement with "paymasters, and collectors of outports" (*The Substance of a Speech delivered in the Irish House of Lords*, Cork, pp. 40–41).

[2] Edward Wakefield's testimony before the Bullion Committee, p. 135. Although Wakefield's statement referred specifically to the time when he testified, the general spirit of his remarks and other evidence strongly suggests that the same situation existed in 1804 and for some years previously.

[3] P. 135.

to recognize that there could be any possible relation between Bank of Ireland note issues and monetary expansion by private banks.

John Puget, in answer to the question: "Has the great increase of Paper issued by the Bank of Ireland since the restriction given a great facility to private Banks in Ireland to increase the issue of their Paper?" replied:

> "I should think not to any great amount; because I do not apprehend that the Bankers keep any excess of Bank of Ireland Paper by them, beyond what they from experience may have found sufficient to support the currency of their own Paper; . . ."[1]

Walter Burrowes said: "I do not think that the issue of National Bank Notes assists in any manner the extension of the issue of private Bankers notes: . . ."[2] Jeremiah D'Olier, imbued with the idea that seems to be held by so many central bankers when criticized for causing inflation in periods of inconvertible paper money, that public "demand" automatically fixes the note circulation at the proper figure as long as banks discount only on sound security, not only denied that Bank of Ireland could exercise any influence over private bank paper, but claimed that private bank issues, if private banks followed a sound credit policy, would simply offset any increases or decreases of Bank of Ireland paper. This view is best given in his own words, in response to the questions put by the Committee:

> "Do you mean then that the sum of Bank of Ireland paper which should be withdrawn would be exactly replaced by the Paper of the private Banks?—I believe it must.
>
> "Do you conceive, that every augmentation of Bank of Ireland Paper produces an exactly proportionate diminution of private Bank Paper, and that every diminution of Bank of Ireland Paper produces an exactly proportionate augmentation of private Bank paper, supposing all other circumstances in the country remain the same?—The general effect will be, that by so much as Bank of Ireland Paper is withdrawn, its place will be supplied by private Bankers Paper, and so *vice versâ*."
>
> . . . .
>
> "Supposing the Bank of Ireland now to diminish its Paper, would not the increased difficulty of obtaining that Paper, operate, in some measure, in the same manner as a difficulty in obtaining Guineas [under cash payments] operated in restraining the disposition to lend in the private Banks?—I think not in any degree whatever."[3]

[1] Pp. 20–21. [2] P. 25. [3] P. 116.

On the other hand, Robert Marshall, the Inspector General of Imports and Exports, took the view that under existing conditions of the private bank paper being "in general considered as good in the event of any disturbances in the country, as the Paper of the Bank of Ireland," it would be possible to have an over-issue of private bank paper even "if there was not an over issue from the Bank of Ireland." However, the general conclusion of his testimony on this point was quite different from that of D'Olier, as in response to the question: "Do you not conceive that the limitation of the Bank of Ireland Paper may have a tendency in some measure to limit the Paper of the private Banks?" he replied: "I apprehend so to a certain extent."[1] John Claudius Beresford, a Dublin banker, who was also a member of the Committee, was the only witness who in response to the question that in almost identical words had been put to five other witnesses: "Do you conceive that the reduction of the quantity of Bank of Ireland Paper has a tendency to reduce the quantity of Paper issued by the private Banks?" gave a categorical answer, "I do."[2]

It is not likely that the Bank of Ireland was as powerless to influence the note issues of private banks as the banking spokesmen would have had the Committee believe. Almost certainly it had some influence on the private bankers, but not as great as modern central banking theory assumes. Perhaps the answer is that there was no fixed relation, and that it may have varied from time to time after 1797, and it may have been different as between banks. Evidence of honest doubt on this point is found in the note that Henry Thornton, presumably at about the same time that the Committee was examining the witnesses, wrote in his copy of Lord King's *Thoughts on the Effects of The Bank Restrictions* opposite King's criticism of the Bank of Ireland for the monetary expansion in Ireland:

> "It ought to be considered on behalf of the Bank of Ireland that the Bank not having the monopoly of the Supply of paper Currency in Dublin (other Bank Paper circulating in the same place) has not the same power which the Bank of England has of limiting the circulation of the country and that the limitation of the Bank of Ireland paper in the present circumstances of Ireland might possibly have little other effect than that of leaving to the other private Banks (which are completely rival Establishments) those profits which the Bank of Ireland should relinquish."[3]

[1] P. 101. [2] P. 95.

[3] *An Enquiry into the Nature and Effects of The Paper Credit of Great Britain*. Edited with an Introduction by F. A. v. Hayek (New York, 1939), p. 319.

The questions on the Bank of Ireland's own credit policy again suggest the hand of Henry Thornton. The Bank of Ireland's discount rate was limited by its charter to 5 per cent. The prevailing rate of discount in Ireland at the time appears to have been 6 per cent. Questions implying that, with the Bank rate under the market rate, the Bank, even though it discounted only good trade bills, could overexpand, were put to many witnesses.[1] This persistent questioning by the Committee brought out little in the way of economic analysis by the witnesses, whose answers frequently were almost meaningless generalities. This is illustrated by the answer of Jeremiah D'Olier, after a long series of questions and answers on the significance of loans by the Bank of Ireland at under the market rate:

> "Do you then admit that the Bank of Ireland is under the necessity of limiting the loans requested by the Merchants and others with a view to the prevention of a too great circulation of Paper, and that it may be necessary not to gratify the wishes of the Public in that respect?—I am perfectly satisfied, that the circulation of the Bank of Ireland is greatly within any necessary restraint of that kind, but I feel that it is the duty of those who conduct the affairs of the Bank to restrain all wanton or unnecessary or unprudent speculation, whether they arise from avarice or folly."[2]

Closely associated with the questioning on the credit policy of the Bank of Ireland with an interest rate under the market rate, were questions as to the relation between note issues and commodity prices.[3] On this point, as on the previous point of the credit policy, the answers were general and inconclusive. No figures were submitted, but two witnesses believed that recently prices of Irish export products had declined, although apparently for reasons independent of the monetary situation.[4] The real result of the cross-examination was to give the members of the Committee the chance to suggest, by skilful questioning, that the credit policy of the Bank of Ireland had made Irish prices higher than they would otherwise have been, and that higher prices in Ireland, through the effect on exports and imports, had depreciated the Irish exchange. An example of this type of question, and of a reply sufficiently eclectic to cover both the price effects and the employment effects of an increased monetary supply, appears in the cross-examination of William Colville:

[1] John Puget, p. 21; Walter Borrowes, p. 24; Jeremiah Harman, p. 38; John Finlay, p. 40; Benjamin Winthrop, p. 43; John Irving, pp. 58–59, 63–64; Jeremiah D'Olier, p. 91.

[2] P. 91. A further extract from D'Olier's evidence on this point is given on pp. 107–109.

[3] John Puget, p. 21; Walter Borrowes, p. 26; Jeremiah Harman, p. 38; John Winthrop, p. 43; Robert Barnewall, pp. 50–51; Jeremiah D'Olier, p. 92; and William Colville, pp. 97–98.

[4] John Irving, p. 64; Robert Barnewall, p. 51.

"Do you then admit that a general augmentation of the circulating medium of a country, whether consisting of Gold only, or of Gold or Paper, or of Paper only, has a tendency to augment the price of articles in exchange for such circulating medium?—It certainly has, unless as the circulating medium augments, that the articles that are to be influenced by it do not augment in an equal proportion."[1]

PROPOSALS FOR EXCHANGE STABILIZATION

The Committee of 1804 had a much simpler task, in presenting a positive programme for the future, than the Bullion Committee had six years later. Exchange rates between Ireland and foreign countries were not involved, nor was the issue of ending the Restriction under consideration. The problem was simply that of the monetary relations, in the absence of specie payments, between two parts of the United Kingdom. Many witnesses were questioned as to the feasibility of a common monetary system for Ireland and England, and the hearings before this Committee are one of the earliest organized discussions of the principles of what today would be called a sterling exchange standard.

James Mansfield, an Edinburgh banker, explained the method by which the exchange between Scotland and England had been stabilized for the previous half century.[2] The leading Edinburgh banks maintained reserves in London and on the basis of these reserves they stood ready to redeem their notes in London funds, and they were also prepared to buy bills on London at a fixed discount. Using this Scotch system as explained by Mansfield as a frame of reference, other witnesses were questioned as to the possibility of using a similar programme to stabilize rates between Dublin and London. The spokesmen for the Bank of Ireland and the Bank of England were united in opposition to any such idea. In the face of a half century of exchange stability between Dublin and London and between Edinburgh and London, and of the continued stability under the Restriction of exchange between Belfast and London, they held that now it would be disastrous, if not impossible, to maintain exchange stability between Dublin and London. The suggestions that the Bank of Ireland be required to redeem in Bank of England notes, that Bank of England notes be made legal tender in Ireland, or that the Bank of Ireland and the Bank of England be consolidated, were all rejected by the banking spokesmen as impractical and dangerous.

[1] P. 97. Further evidence of Colville, reprinted on pp. 101–106, and the evidence of Robert Barnewall, reprinted on pp. 96–98, illustrate the type of leading questions put to witnesses on the relation of note issues, prices and exchange rates.

[2] Pp. 32–33, 52–56. Mansfield's evidence is reprinted in part on pp. 91–95.

The implicit theoretical premise of their opposition was that exchange rates are the result entirely of trade and capital movements, and that central bank policy is powerless to affect exchange rates by affecting the balance of payments. This was supplemented by some curious ideas as to the peculiar conditions that were supposed to exist between Dublin and London. Benjamin Winthrop, the Deputy Governor of the Bank of England, pointed to "a great distinction of country; the sea goes between them; they have a different Treasury, a different Bank, and an Exchange between the countries has always existed."[1] William Colville denied that the exchange situation between Edinburgh and London had any relevance to the Irish problem and pointed to the balance of remittances from Ireland as making impractical any common medium of exchange,[2] or any union of the banks of England and Ireland. Jeremiah D'Olier took essentially the same position.[3] John Puget pictured the Bank as facing ruin if required to redeem in Bank of England notes.[4]

A number of witnesses, however, were more favourable to the idea of unifying the currencies of England and Ireland. Even those who, like Walter Borrowes[5] and John Irving,[6] had claimed that the issues of the Bank of Ireland had not caused a depreciation of the Irish currency, admitted under cross-examination that a policy of redemption of notes in London exchange, either with or without a consolidation of the Banks, would permit a stable exchange rate.[7] An interesting variation of the stabilization proposals was the suggestion of Thomas Thorpe Frank to make the public debt of Ireland payable at a fixed rate in both Ireland and England, and of John Claudius Beresford that the interest on the public debt of both Ireland and England be "payable at the Bank of either, at the option of the holder."

The procedure of the Irish Treasury in transferring its loans from England to Ireland involved some fundamental issues of exchange stabilization, in particular as to the effect upon the market rate of intermittent sales of exchange to a few individuals at less than the market rate. The full implications of this problem were not explored. Apparently it had aroused the interest of the Committee primarily because of the

[1] P. 45. [2] Pp. 120–121. [3] Pp. 113–117.

[4] "Do you conceive that if the Bank of Ireland were compelled to pay in Bank of England notes or Exchequer Bills, it would tend to lower the rate of Exchange?—It certainly would lower the rate of Exchange, and their property at the same time."

"What do you conceive to be the objections to such a measure being adopted?—If the balance of debt should continue against Ireland, ultimately the ruin of the Bank, by its paying the whole loss of the Exchange of the country." P. 121.

[5] P. 23. [6] P. 58.

[7] Walter Borrowes, p. 27; William Coningham, pp. 56–58; John Irving pp. 59, 62–63; John Roach, p. 82; John Claudius Beresford, p. 95; Thomas Thorpe Frank, pp. 112–113. A portion of Irving's evidence on exchange stabilization is reprinted on pp. 99–100.

possible favouritism involved rather than because of its bearing on the principles of exchange stabilization. Indirectly, however, the evidence showed the futility, from a public point of view, of isolated sales of exchange at under the market rate.[1]

The cross-examination of several witnesses also raised the question as to whether responsibility for exchange policy should rest with the Bank of Ireland or with the Irish Treasury.[2] As a summary of the larger policy issues involved in the relations between Treasury and Central Bank, the thousands of pages that have appeared on this topic in the past century and a half have added little to the succinct statement of the problem in the questioning of John Puget and his reply. After discussion of a proposal that the Bank of Ireland participate in the transfer of government funds to Ireland, this dialogue followed:

> "Would it not throw the power of fixing the rate of Exchange on the Bank of Ireland?—Certainly, so far as it goes."
> "Is that more natural to a commercial country than leaving the power in the Treasury?—That depends very much on the use each would make of it."[3]

REPORT OF THE COMMITTEE

The hearings extended from March 5 to May 9, 1804, with a break from March 28 to April 10. The Minutes of Evidence and Appendixes were reported to the House of Commons from time to time in May. On June 13 the Report of the Committee was submitted to the Commons, and on June 19 was ordered to be printed. Its 23 folio pages were written in a concise and clear-cut style that contrasts with the prolixity of the Bullion Report. It divided the problem of the exchange rate between Ireland and England into three parts:

1. "As to the Fact of an unfavourable Exchange existing, and to what Extent;
2. As to the Causes which have created it;
3. As to the Remedies which can be resorted to for either removing or alleviating the Inconveniences arising from it."[4]

[1] See the cross-examination of James Crofton, Chief Clerk of The Irish Treasury, pp. 66–71; and Appendix No. 4, "Memorandum to be laid before the Committee of the House of Commons appointed to enquire into the State of Ireland with respect to the Exchange, & with the Book kept at the Irish Treasury, wherein the Application for Drafts on England are entered."

[2] John Puget, pp. 34–35, 125–127; John Irving, p. 59; John Roach, pp. 81–82; William Colville, p. 122; Jeremiah D'Olier, p. 123. A portion of D'Olier's evidence on this point is reprinted on pp. 109–110; a portion of Puget's evidence is reprinted on pp. 118–121.

[3] P. 34.

[4] P. 1.

As to the facts of exchange there was no dispute. The Irish paper currency for several years had been at a discount in terms of London exchange, but in Belfast, where gold was the common circulating medium, the currency was at a small premium in terms of London exchange. Furthermore, guineas were at a premium in Dublin, and this premium corresponded closely to the difference between the Belfast-London rate and the Dublin-London rate.[1]

This difference between the Dublin-London rate and the Belfast-London rate enabled the Committee to develop clearly the distinction between the real exchange and the nominal exchange. By the real exchange it meant the rate in terms of the same monetary standard, that is, gold or Irish bank notes redeemable in gold. By the nominal exchange it meant the rate in terms of the monetary standard currently used in quoting exchange. Although the Committee did not go into any extended analysis of the theoretical significance of the distinction between the real and nominal rates, the clear implication was that the real exchange reflected the effect of unilateral transfers, of shifts in the terms of trade, and of structural changes in trade, and that the nominal exchange reflected these changes as well as the changes in the monetary standard.

The Committee reached the conclusion, on the basis of the Belfast-London rate, that the real exchange was favourable to Ireland, a view which it believed was supported by the statistics of the Irish balance of payments. It said that the Restriction on cash payments had permitted a monetary expansion, and "that this depreciation in Ireland arises almost entirely, if not solely, from an excess of Paper, appears highly probable." The Committee's belief that the Restriction had permitted a large expansion in the total means of payment in Ireland undoubtedly was correct. However, its conclusion that the exchange situation between Dublin and London, under existing trade and loan conditions, could only be explained in terms of a monetary expansion by the Bank of Ireland, rested upon general analysis rather than upon statistical evidence. The Report gives the figures for the issues of the Bank of Ireland, and the Dublin-London

[1] The Committee assumed that the Bank of England note was still at a parity with the guinea, at least in Ireland, although a small premium had been paid for guineas in England (Testimony of Walter Borrowes, p. 28), for after speaking of the premium on guineas in terms of Bank of Ireland notes, it adds ". . . but further, the circulating Paper of Ireland seems equally depreciated when compared with a Bank of England Note; . . ." This corresponds with the testimony of John Puget (p. 23). It also is in line with the testimony of Thomas Thorpe Frank (p. 109), and with the figures submitted by him (Appendix I) covering the period 1799–March 1804, which show that the premium on guineas in Dublin generally was no greater, and sometimes was less, than the Dublin premium on London exchange.

In Newry, a town about halfway between Dublin and Belfast, London exchange was quoted in terms both of bank notes and of specie. Figures for 1803 and the first three months of 1804 show the difference in the price of London exchange, in the two currencies, as very close to the difference between the Belfast-London rate and the Dublin-London rate, and also to the specie premium in Dublin.

exchange, for March 1797, April 1801, and January 1, 1804, and states that "a strong presumption arises of the connexion between an increased Issue and a high Exchange." These figures, however, are not in themselves convincing evidence, as other dates could be picked when there was no relation, or an inverse relation, between changes in the circulation of the Bank of Ireland and in the exchange rate on London.

It is likely, in view of what is known of the Irish monetary situation, and of general statements made in the hearings about commodity prices, that prices of products bought and sold in England, as well as prices of domestically traded products, had risen in Ireland as compared with England. The Committee, however, presented no figures to support such a conclusion. The Committee's discussion of the price situation was, except for the tacit assumption that the exchange situation was the result of relatively higher prices in Ireland than in England, limited to a reference to "the over-abundant issue which has caused the depreciation of Paper in general, enhancing thereby the price of the necessaries of life, and of all manufactures."

The implicit assumptions of the Committee as to the relation between exchange rates and prices in Ireland come out most clearly in its analysis of the effect of the exchange rate upon the absentee landlords. Apparently the rents of all properties were fixed in terms of Irish currency. Proposals for penalizing the absentee were of long standing, and in February, 1797, only a few days before the Restriction, the Irish House of Commons had debated at length a bill imposing a tax of 2s. on the pound on all rents paid to persons who lived out of Ireland more than six months in the year, and had defeated the bill by a vote of 122-49.[1] The effect of the depreciation of the Dublin-London exchange upon the absentee landlord was not a simple matter. It depended upon the medium in which the absentee received his Irish rents, and upon the change in the relation between Irish prices of the products and services that would be bought by a resident landlord, and the English prices of the products and services bought by the absentee landlord, as compared with the change in the Irish-English exchange rate. The Committee said on this problem:

> ". . . [the Committee] wish to observe upon an opinion entertained by some of the witnesses, that the present high Exchange operates as a tax upon Absentees, and is in effect a bounty on export, and a discouragement to import. If the real exchange were unfavourable to Ireland the opinion might have some foundation; but if it be, as it has been already suggested, in favour of Ireland, the Absentee who receives his Rents in Guineas has a gain instead of a loss on the remittance;

[1] *Parliamentary Register*. Vol. 17, pp. 378–403. February 28, 1797.

a fact which is felt and acknowledged by all proprietors in those districts where rents are so paid. On the other hand, if the rates of the nominal Exchange against Ireland arise from the depreciation of the circulating Paper there, that depreciation must equally affect the resident and the absent proprietor; the difference is, that the Absentee sees the depreciation reduced to an item in his account, when the Paper is to be converted for him into the Currency of another country, but it operates on the Resident, by raising the price of every thing, and though he feels the effect, yet its operation is so blended with the price that it does not present itself ostensibly."[1]

The Committee pointed out that a repeal of the Restriction would restore a common circulating medium but made no recommendation on this issue, and sagely remarked that "its continuance may be connected with political considerations, the discussion of which would involve your Committee in a very extended and tedious Inquiry." But it strongly recommended that the Bank of Ireland take steps to redeem its notes in Bank of England notes or in London funds, and though it suggested that the proceeds of Irish borrowing in London might be used to create a stabilization fund, it pointed out that any permanent stabilization must be related to the credit policy of the Bank of Ireland.

The closing section of the Report dealt with the "current Coin of Ireland." The Committee made a few recommendations on the details of coinage, but it stressed the idea that any permanent relief of the shortage of good silver coin must be found in a stabilization of the exchange rate.

> This evil is clearly to be traced to the unfavourable Exchange . . . [Your Committee] . . . cannot conclude this branch of their subject without remarking that the state of the Silver Coinage of Ireland, and the circumstances which have attended it, form an additional argument in favour of those measures for rectifying and fixing the Exchange which they have recommended in the preceding part of this Report.

The Report received no immediate attention in Parliament, and not until five years later was even an attempt made to have it discussed. A plausible explanation for this lack of current interest in the issues of monetary and foreign exchange policy presented in the Report is to be found in the small coin crisis in Ireland in March and April, 1804; in the great improvement in the Dublin-London exchange between April and September, 1804; and probably also in the discontinuance of the practice, which had played so important a part in the earlier Parlia-

[1] Presumably the witnesses referred to by the Committee were John Winthrop, p. 44, and William Colville, p. 119.

mentary debate on the Irish exchange, of paying Irish officials in English currency at the par of exchange.

THE SMALL COIN CRISIS IN IRELAND

The situation of the silver coin of Ireland had been getting steadily worse for several years before 1804. Of full weight silver there was virtually none. Clipped and abraded coins, counterfeit coins, silver notes, and I.O.U.'s circulated side by side at parity, in a live-and-let-live spirit. The counterfeits had been given *de facto* legal tender status by the willingness of the Government offices to accept them, and by the practice of army paymasters of using them to pay troops. Suddenly in the latter part of March, 1804, apparently as the result of the decision of the Post Office no longer to receive counterfeit coin,[1] not only did counterfeit coin lose its currency, but in the general uncertainty as to what coins were acceptable, retail trade was practically at a standstill. The theory and practice of exchange stabilization, which the Committee was discussing in London, must have seemed at the moment a remote theme to most of the people of Ireland, worried as to whether the coin in their pockets was worth anything. The Candid Cobler's letter of March 17, 1804, is probably a fair summary of the situation:

> ". . . breweries, distilleries, flour mills, even *chandlery*—have their paper issues, (not tokens to pay their workmen) but banking notes *unstampt*, to extend their credit and create capital:—how this may end, Heaven knows! but it is of more immediate consequence to us individually, than the price of Bullion, or the exchange to Hamburgh.
>
> We are at this moment arrived at the period of abuse in coinage that articles in detail (if they do not form an aggregate nearly to a pound note) cannot be purchased; for the trader will not accept the coin tendered, nor the consumer the change offered; . . ."[2]

Officials of the Irish Government[3] were fearful lest the coinage crisis should become the occasion for riots and rebellion in a country that

[1] The Earl of Hardwicke, Lord Lieutenant of Ireland, wrote on March 31, 1804: "I must here observe that it has been stated to me that the instructions given by the Post Office to their collectors in the course of the last week, to reject all the counterfeit coin which had formerly been received, contributed very much to the general stoppage of the circulation." B. M., Add. Ms. 35, 747, f. 290.

[2] *Op. cit.*, p. 24.

[3] The papers of the Earl of Hardwicke, the Minute Book of the Bank of Ireland, and the Dublin and provincial Irish newspapers in the period of the Committee hearings, all show great concern over the state of the silver coin and the small notes, but have almost no references to the exchange situation. In the Hardwicke papers (B. M., Add. Ms. 35, 748, f. 25) is the Report of a Select Committee appointed by a Committee of Merchants of the City of Cork "for the purpose of inquiring into the present state of the Paper Circulation." The Report denounced the abuses of silver notes, bad silver, bad bankers, and the "species of swindling circulation termed I.O.U.", but made only a passing reference to the exchange rate, which apparently seemed like a minor annoyance as compared with these other problems.

currently had a high propensity to engage in such activities. The Lord Lieutenant wrote on March 28, 1804, that the inconvenience over the silver currency "has increased to an alarming degree, and has created a very serious clamour in the City."[1] On the same day a clergyman in Drogheda wrote to the Government, "To my certain knowledge, numbers of poor creatures were obliged to go without food on Saturday and Sunday as neither Baker nor Meat Monger would take the silver they had to offer."[2] The appearance of an anonymous broadside headed "Bad Silver" was further evidence of the seriousness of the situation:

> "Hunger and Starving for want of Bread—can't get Provisions, nor Coals for our Families. Fellow Citizens and Soldiers let us go to the Banks and tear open the Chests where there is plenty of Gold and Silver and let us not tamely submit to see our Children perish for want of Bread. Who can blame us."[3]

The unwillingness of the British Government, despite the urging by the authorities in Dublin, to rescind its order against the acceptance of counterfeits which had so long passed current made it difficult to straighten out matters in Dublin.[4]

By the middle of April the coinage situation had improved. A more liberal interpretation on the part of the Government as to what coins were acceptable eased matters, the legalistic position on counterfeit coin was modified to the extent of reimbursing soldiers for counterfeit silver given to them by paymasters,[5] and arrangement was made with the Bank of Ireland to retire from circulation counterfeit silver.[6] Silver tokens were put in circulation in several smaller towns and one bank in Dublin issued silver notes.[7] Soon afterwards the Bank of Ireland issued tokens, in the form of Spanish dollars and half-dollars, over-stamped with the head of King George, to pass at 6 shillings to the dollar. The Irish coin situation after the middle of April, although far from ideal, at least permitted retail trade to function once more.

[1] B. M., Add. Ms. 35, 747, f. 254.

[2] B. M., Add. Ms. 35, 747, f. 261.

[3] B. M., Add. Ms. 35, 747, f. 296.

[4] A memorandum of Lord Liverpool, dated April 5, 1804, took the view that the Government would under no circumstances accept counterfeit coin. It is not clear whether Liverpool realized that the Government offices in Dublin for some time previous had been accepting and paying out counterfeit coin, and that probably a substantial part of the coin circulating in Dublin before March, 1804, was counterfeit. Add. Ms. 35, 748, ff. 124–133.

[5] B. M., Add. Ms. 35, 748, f. 53.

[6] The Bank, after conversations with the Government, agreed to buy up "adulterated silver . . . for a certain period at a certain value," (Minute Book of Bank of Ireland, April 3, 1804), but resolved (*Ibid.*, April 14, 1804) that "The Clerks be instructed to reject any pieces which appear to be composed of Base Metal only, or to be highly adulterated."

[7] B. M., Add. Ms. 35, 748, ff. 155, 182.

IMPROVEMENT IN THE IRISH EXCHANGE

When John Foster moved for the appointment of the Committee on March 2, 1804, the Dublin-London rate in London was 18¼, representing a depreciation of nearly 10 per cent, but the Irish pound improved after the first part of April. On June 1 the rate was 14, in September it went to 12½, but in October rose to 15. In December 1804 the rate fell to 11, and early in January 1805 to 9¾.[1]

It seems clear that this improvement in the Irish exchange at the end of 1804 was the result of Treasury drawings to transfer from London to Dublin the proceeds of an Irish loan, but it appears that the transfer was made in a haphazard way, and probably in large part below the market rates. The Irish Treasury in December 1804 offered bills on London, for any sums over £10, at 11½, subsequently offered bills at 10, and then at par. Lord Archibald Hamilton criticized the drawing of bills by the Treasury at par on the grounds that it only operated "as a bounty to the merchants in whose favour the bills were drawn."[2]

John Foster, in defence of Treasury exchange operations of a type that had been so recently criticized by the Committee of which he was Chairman, said

> "The lords of the treasury applied in the first instance to the bank of Ireland, for this purpose, considering them, as the most proper body to bring the money over. The bank however, refused to interfere, from an apprehension, that as many of the directors were engaged in the business of exchange, any act which would have the effect of constituting them arbitrators of exchange, might draw upon their court of directors, odium and reprobation."[3]

He said that of £200,000 originally offered at 11½, of a balance of over £1 million to be transferred, only £170,000 was taken; that when the rate was reduced to 11 and £200,000 more was offered, only £170,000 was taken; and that the Lords of the Treasury "therefore, considered that to secure purchasers for the whole sums wanted, the exchange should be still further lowered, and in consequence they reduced it to par."

Despite Foster's claim that it was necessary to reduce the rate to par in order to transfer the loan to Ireland, it seems clear that the matter was handled ineptly, and that even if no favouritism was involved, as had

[1] It is probable that there were occasions when the actual rate was even lower than the quoted rate. In the House of Commons on March 21, 1805, Sir William Pulteney stated that Bank of England notes were at a 3 per cent discount in Ireland. Hansard, First Series, Vol. IV, pp. 71–72.

[2] Hansard, First Series, Vol. III, Feb. 5, 1805, pp. 259–260.

[3] *Ibid.*, p. 260.

almost certainly been the case in earlier drawings by the Treasury, the result had been that the Treasury got fewer Irish pounds and that there was only a temporary improvement in the Irish exchange. Under the circumstance it is likely that Lord Archibald Hamilton's charge is correct, that when the Treasury offered £150,000 in exchange at par

> ". . . the sum of £500,000 was subscribed; and such was the eagerness and avidity to procure a share of it, that a kind of riot had taken place amongst the bidders at the castle, which required the military to suppress."[1]

Hamilton introduced a resolution "expressing disapprobation of the conduct of the Irish treasury" in selling bills on London "at rates inferior to those at which they had been before sold."[2] In the debate that followed, Henry Thornton made the pertinent observation that:

> "it was not the manner of passing the bills, but the quantity in the market, which was the occasion of the increase or depreciation of the rate of exchange."[3]

Thornton, however, opposed Hamilton's motion, although his remarks suggest that he did not approve of the Treasury action, but that he felt that a disapproval of the Treasury practice did not deal with the basic difficulty of the Irish exchange. He "was surprised" that the Bank of Ireland "had not taken the hint given in the report of the committee." The resolution of Hamilton was defeated.

No information is available as to the relative roles of the Treasury and of the Bank of Ireland in the exchange market during the remaining years of the Restriction, but in view of the fact that there was no further Parliamentary criticism of the Treasury, even from those hardy critics of Irish monetary policy, Lord Archibald Hamilton, Henry Parnell, and Lord Henry Petty,[4] it is a reasonable surmise that the Treasury did not repeat the disorderly transfers that it had made in 1804 and 1805. There is also no direct evidence that the Bank of Ireland formally accepted any of the criticisms that the Committee of 1804 made of its credit operations. However, the less liberal credit policy of the Bank after 1803,[5] the improvement in Irish exchange, and its narrow movements between 1805 and 1813 all suggest that the Bank of Ireland had heeded the Committee's criticisms and suggestions. It is not likely that for a period of

[1] Hansard, Vol. IV, March 21, 1805, p. 67. [2] *Ibid.*, p. 68. [3] *Ibid.*, p. 72.

[4] Petty went to the House of Lords in 1809 as the third Marquis of Lansdowne.

[5] Notes (exclusive of post bills), which had reached a high of £2,636,316 at the end of 1803, declined to under £2 million in 1807 and 1808, and did not again reach the 1803 figure until the end of 1811.

eight years purely "natural forces" would have limited exchange fluctuations under unconvertible paper to a range that never exceeded 5 per cent. The ability of the Bank of Ireland to control the monetary situation in Ireland was also increased by the outlawing of notes of private banks of under £1 by the law of May 17, 1805,[1] and by the great reduction in the issue of private tokens, although the latter were not outlawed until 1812.[2]

While the Committee was holding its hearings, Lord Archibald Hamilton introduced a motion condemning the practice of paying at par Irish civil officers resident in Ireland, but the motion was defeated by a vote of 82–44 after a sharp debate.[3] Henry Thornton in the debate showed his usual concern with the economic principles involved, rather than with the issues out of which political capital could be made, by his observation:

> "It would be better to apply the time of the house in devising a remedy for the radical evil, the present rate of exchange between this country and Ireland."[4]

After the defeat of Hamilton's motion of censure, I find no mention either in Parliament or elsewhere of payments of Irish officials at the par of exchange.[5] However, there is circumstantial evidence that the practice was not continued. Although Hamilton's motion of criticism was voted down, those who held the majority view were on the defensive, and supported their position on technical legal grounds rather than on grounds of public policy. Lord Archibald Hamilton and Henry Parnell continued their criticism of the Irish monetary situation until the end of the Restriction and it is unlikely that they would have let pass the opportunity to take the Government to task for such remittances at par, especially in 1815, 1816, and 1819, years when the Irish pound was at a discount of from 4 to 10 per cent.

PARLIAMENTARY ACTION ON IRISH MONETARY SITUATION: 1805–1816

The first and the only time that any attempt was made in Parliament to consider the Report was in April, 1809, when Henry Parnell moved that the House resolve itself into a Committee of the Whole to consider the Report of The Irish Currency Committee. He stated that he intended, if this were done, to submit a Resolution "That it is expedient that the

[1] 45 G. III, Part ii, c. 41. [2] 52 G. III, c. 157.

[3] Hansard, First Series, Vol. II, p. 126. April 12, 1804.

[4] *Ibid.*, p. 123.

[5] A search in the British Treasury records from 1805 to 1816 reveals no clear evidence either that the practice had been continued or had been stopped.

Coin of the United Kingdom shall be of the same standard and value as the Coin now is of Great Britain."[1] In an able statement he explained how the Bank of Ireland would use its London balances to stabilize the rate, and pointed out that with the exchange practically at par[2] this was a particularly opportune time to put such a plan into effect. He received almost no support for his motion, which both John Foster and Henry Thornton opposed, and it was defeated without a division.[3]

In 1809 and 1810, when the Irish exchange was close to a parity with London, the controversy over the English monetary situation, and over the policy of the Bank of England, developed in England. The rising price of gold and silver, and the declining value of English currency in terms of Hamburg exchange, were the occasion for Ricardo's first efforts as an economist, and led to the appointment in February, 1810 of the Bullion Committee. The terms of reference of the Bullion Committee did not call for any investigation of the exchange situation between England and Ireland. Nevertheless, a substantial amount of information on the Irish situation was brought out in the Evidence and in the Exhibits, and the Bullion Report has an extended reference to the Irish situation.[4] This familiarity of the drafters of the Bullion Report with the Irish monetary situation in 1803 and 1804 is in contrast with Ricardo's failure to make any reference to the Irish monetary situation in his published writings in 1809–1811, and with his apparent lack of familiarity with the Irish situation as it might bear on the gold premium in England.[5]

The Bullion Committee, probably because the Dublin-London exchange had been so close to par for several years, made no separate recommendations on the Irish Restriction, other than a general statement which showed a confusion in the minds of the members of the Committee as to the provisions of the Restriction legislation:

[1] Hansard, First Series, Vol. XIV, pp. 75–77.

[2] The London-Dublin rate on April 18, 1809, was 8¾.

[3] *Ibid.*, pp. 90–91. Thornton said in opposition "that he was a member of the committee to which the hon. gent. had referred, but when the Committee recommended the measure he had quoted, they had a view to an antecedent measure, which did not take place." It is not certain what Thornton meant by "an antecedent measure," but possibly he referred to the building up by the Bank of Ireland of an exchange stabilization fund in London.

[4] The section of the Bullion Report dealing with Ireland is reprinted on pp. 122–124.

[5] In his second letter to the *Morning Chronicle*, Ricardo wrote: "The severity of the law against the exportation of gold coin, prevents *any* one from openly selling bank-notes at a discount . . . from the fear that as it is known that no one can purchase guineas but with a view to exportation, he would become an object of suspicion . . ." *The Works and Correspondence of David Ricardo.* (Cambridge, 1951), Vol. III, p. 24.
Until 1812 guineas were generally and openly used in payments in Northern Ireland, prices there were higher in terms of bank notes than in terms of gold, there was an open and legal premium on gold in Ireland, and there was no prohibition on the shipment of gold from England to Ireland. Hence there was a good economic reason in England to pay a premium for guineas for legal use.

"It will be convenient also for the Chartered Banks of Ireland and Scotland, and all the Country Banks, that they should not be compelled to pay in specie until some time after the resumption of payments in Cash by the Bank of England; but that they continue for a short period upon their present basis, of being liable to pay their own notes on demand in Bank of England paper."[1]

The Bullion Committee was in error on two points: the Restriction legislation had not relieved the Chartered Banks of Scotland or any country banks of the obligation to pay in specie, although in practice they had not been required to pay, nor was the Bank of Ireland "liable" under the Restriction legislation to pay its notes in Bank of England paper.

The use of gold in Northern Ireland declined somewhat after 1808, but the continued insistence of a few landlords on receiving guineas again brought the Irish monetary situation to the attention of Parliament in 1811 and 1812 in connection with Lord Stanhope's Gold Coin Bill. The practice, long common in the North of Ireland, of openly paying a premium for British gold, had spread to Great Britain in 1809 and 1810. The third of Vansittart's resolutions in opposition to the Bullion Report:

"That the promissory notes of the said Company [the Bank of England] have hitherto been, and are at this time, held in public estimation to be equivalent to the legal coin of the realm, and generally accepted as such in all pecuniary transactions to which such coin is lawfully applicable."[2]

was not a true statement of prevailing conditions in England at the time it was passed in June, 1811. Lord King's famous order, apparently taken in retaliation against this Resolution, that his tenants pay him in gold, led to the passage of the Gold Coin Bill, intended to compel creditors and landlords to accept bank notes at par. The bill, as passed in July, 1811, did not apply to Ireland, and the practice of demanding payment in gold was still followed by some of the landlords of Ulster. The next year the Gold Coin Act was strengthened to prevent Lord King from taking advantage of a loophole in it, and was amended to apply to Ireland, which in effect made Bank of Ireland notes legal tender throughout Ireland.[3]

Henry Parnell, during the debates in April, 1812, on the extension of the Gold Coin Act, had moved that further proceedings on the bill be

[1] P. 33.

[2] Hansard, First Series, Vol. XX., p. 70.

[3] The details of this controversy over gold payments are given in my "Legal Tender During the English and Irish Bank Restrictions," pp. 245–250.

postponed "for the purpose of appointing a select committee to enquire into the state of the currency in Ireland."[1] In the debate that followed, several members referred to the Irish Currency Report of 1804, but there was no general support for Parnell's motion. The failure to take any action on Parnell's motion marked the end of any Parliamentary efforts, before the Restriction was finally lifted, to give further consideration to the monetary situation in Ireland. The Irish pound, that had been at a premium in terms of London exchange during most of the time from November 1812 to May 1815, depreciated rapidly in the latter months of 1815 and the early months of 1816. In January 1816 the rate reached 18, which had been exceeded for only a few months in 1803 and 1804. Yet there was no move, either in or out of Parliament, to call on the Government or the Bank of Ireland for an explanation or to make a political issue of the depreciation of the Dublin exchange. In contrast with the flood of publications provoked by the depreciation of 1803 and 1804, no pamphleteer discussed the Irish exchange in the period after Waterloo. One reason for this difference between 1815–1816 and 1803–1804 may have been the absence of any transfers at par from Irish currency into English currency for the benefit of favoured officials, thus eliminating a situation that had done so much to stimulate the investigation of 1804. Another probable explanation, based on more solid economic grounds, is that the exchange depreciation of 1815 and 1816 came at a time of economic distress and sharply falling agricultural prices in Ireland. The depreciation of exchange undoubtedly meant that Irish agricultural prices were higher, and the Irish monetary circulation larger, than had the Irish pound been held at parity with London.[2] Under such conditions the depreciation of the Irish pound must have appeared as a blessing that gave some small relief in a period of economic distress.

RESUMPTION OF CASH PAYMENTS IN 1821

Between 1814 and 1821 English monetary policy, and particularly the question of the resumption of specie payments by the Bank of England, was vigorously debated both in and out of Parliament. The various legislative acts extending the Restriction on the Bank of England had companion measures extending the Restriction on the Bank of Ireland until

[1] Hansard, First Series, Vol. XXII, p. 279.

[2] Silberling's index of the annual average of the cost of living in England is:

1813 . .	187	1816 . .	135
1814 . .	176	1817 . .	151
1815 . .	150		

Op. cit., p. 235.
His index of commodity prices shows an even sharper drop between 1814 and 1816. P. 232.

three months after the resumption of payments by the Bank of England.[1] But virtually no attention was given to the Irish monetary situation, and the legislation relating to the Bank of Ireland provoked almost no Parliamentary discussion. It seemed to have been assumed that the policy established for the Bank of England would apply to the Bank of Ireland, and the niceties of the additional problem that the Bank of Ireland faced in bringing its notes to parity with the Bank of England note, and the question of ending the anomalous 13 to 12 par ratio between the Irish pound and the English pound, were ignored.

In February 1819 the Committees of Secrecy of The Lords and of The Commons started hearings on the "Expediency of The Resumption of Cash Payments" by the Bank of England, and these hearings reflected the same attitude of virtually ignoring the special problem of Ireland. No Irish witnesses gave evidence before the Commons Committee, but the Committee said in the Second Report of May 6, 1819 that they:

> "have the satisfaction of stating to the House, on the authority of the Governor of the Bank of Ireland, whom they have had the opportunity of personally examining, that there is reason to believe that no difficulty would exist, on the part of the Bank of Ireland, in carrying into effect, any regulations of the same nature with those which may be adopted with respect to the Bank of England."[2]

The Lords Committee on April 8, 1819, almost at the end of its hearings, called Thomas Bainbridge of Puget, Bainbridge, and Co.[3] Bainbridge's brief testimony dealt in large part with the details of his gold transactions for the Bank of Ireland. He was also questioned about the recent rise in Dublin-London exchange.[4] This he attributed to large purchases by Irish residents of British Government Stock to take advantage of recent legislation enabling "individuals to transfer Stock from the English Funds to the Irish Funds" on particularly favourable terms, and to "the greater Amount of Rents remitted to Landlords resident here from Ireland in the last Year, arising, as I have been informed, from Arrears, in many Instances, having been paid up."

Nathaniel Sneyd, Governor of the Bank of Ireland and a member of

[1] 54 G. III, c. 130, July 25, 1814; 55 G. III, c. 41, May 2, 1815; 56 G. III, c. 48, June 20, 1816; 58 G. III, c. 60, June 1, 1818.

[2] *Reports from the Secret Committee on The Expediency of The Bank Resuming Cash Payments*. 1819, p. 18.

[3] *Reports Respecting The Bank of England Resuming Cash Payments. Communicated* by the Lords, 12th May 1819. *Ordered by* The House of Commons, to be Printed 12 *May*, 1819. Pp. 259–262.

[4] The rate in early January 1818 was 9; it had risen to 10½ by February 1819; was 12½ when he testified; and early in May 1819 it rose to 15.

the Currency Committee of 1804, and James M'Call, a Director of the Bank of Ireland, who were the last witnesses called by the Committee, also said the principal cause of the rise in the Dublin-London exchange was the transfer of Government stock to Ireland,[1] but said that Absentee Remittances were an additional reason for the rise of exchange.

The Bank of Ireland, like the Bank of England, had, when the price of gold was close to the mint par and the Dublin-London rate close to par,[2] redeemed in gold some older notes and small denomination notes.[3] Both the Lords and Commons Committees issued preliminary Reports criticizing this practice of partial gold redemption by the Bank of England, in advance of a general resumption of payments. Parliament acted promptly and forbade the Bank of England[4] and the Bank of Ireland[5] to redeem any notes in gold, no matter what the denomination or the date of issue. Several members of the Commons criticized the taking of action in regard to the Bank of Ireland on the basis of a report that related only to the Bank of England, and Sir Henry Parnell[6] said that "it would almost appear that the Committee on Bank affairs had wholly forgotten those of the Bank of Ireland, since no mention was made of them by any member of the committee."[7] But again, the Government's policy prevailed of giving no separate consideration to the Irish situation.

Three months later, on July 2, 1819, Parliament extended the Restriction on the Bank of England to May 1, 1823, but provided that payments in gold bullion, at the rate of £4–1s. per oz., were to start on February 1, 1820, and the basis of redemption was to be liberalized by stages, until all restrictions on payment in coin were to be lifted on May 1, 1823.[8] This was followed by companion legislation governing the Bank of Ireland; redemption on gold bullion was to start on April 5,

[1] *Ibid.*, p. 269. They estimated that £3,600,000 had been transferred for the purchase of stock. Thomas Bainbridge had estimated transfers for this purpose at "more than Four Millions." P. 261.

[2] The rate in London did not go above 9 between September 30, 1817, and March 19, 1818.

[3] The only information that I can find on the extent of such gold redemptions by the Bank of Ireland is in the testimony of Sneyd and M'Call before the Lords Committee of Secrecy of 1819:

"2. Has the Bank of Ireland ever given any Notice to pay in Cash any of its Notes?
Yes; similar Notices to those given by the Bank of England.
3. Can you state what Proportion the Notes, of which Notice was given to pay in Cash, bore to the whole Amount of outstanding Notes?
We cannot.
(Governor). I should think it very inconsiderable."

Op. cit., p. 267.

[4] 59 G. III, c. 23, April 6, 1819.

[5] 59 G. III, c. 24, April 8, 1819.

[6] Parnell had succeeded to the baronetcy in 1812.

[7] Hansard, First Series, Vol. XXXIX, p. 1423. April 6, 1818.

[8] 59 G. III, c. 49, July 2, 1819.

1820, and thereafter each step was to be taken one month after the Bank of England, with full redemption in coin to begin on June 2, 1823.[1] The Parliamentary records give no hint as to why resumption by the Bank of Ireland was postponed beyond that by the Bank of England. The report of the debates on the Bank of England Restriction Act covers over 125 pages in Hansard, but there was no separate discussion of the Bank of Ireland Restriction Act. There is no record, either in the Committee hearings, in the documents in the Appendix of The Committee Reports, or in the Parliamentary debates, that any information as to the reserves of the Bank of Ireland, either gold or London funds, or the loans of the Bank of Ireland to Government, were ever furnished to the Government, or even asked for. The contrast is striking between the elaborate data that Parliament demanded on the Bank of England and the detailed consideration that it gave to the ability of the Bank to resume and maintain gold payments, and the apparent failure of Parliament to get any information about the condition of the Bank of Ireland before providing for the resumption of payments in Ireland.

While the bill for the resumption of cash payments by the Bank of England was before Parliament, Sir Henry Parnell proposed "a measure for assimilating the currency of Ireland to the currency of England, and for better regulating the exchanges between the two countries," and moved for the appointment of a Committee to inquire into the matter.[2] He withdrew his motion when Nicholas Vansittart, the Chancellor of the Exchequer, suggested that it would not be feasible "to go into a committee" at that time, and said that he would support a motion for the appointment of such a Committee at the next session, "unless some very unforeseen occurrence took place."[3]

In 1820 there was an improvement in the Dublin exchange. The rate in London had been 11½ in January; it had fallen to 9 by the end of March, to 8 by the middle of June, and to 6¼ by October. Gold bars in London fell to the mint price of £3–17–10½ in December 1820, and remained at this figure throughout 1821.[4] The Bank of Ireland note was at a premium in terms of gold. Ireland had suffered a series of bank failures in 1820, and the Bank of Ireland, for reasons that are not clear, had contributed to the monetary stringency by restricting its credits.[5] It was

[1] 59 G. III, c. 99. July 12, 1819.

[2] Hansard, First Series, Vol. XL, pp. 1194–5, June 16, 1819. [3] *Ibid.*, p. 1195.

[4] *Report from the Committee of Secrecy on The Bank of England Charter, with The Minutes of Evidence, Appendix and Index.* 1832. Appendix, No. 96.

[5] The total note circulation (exclusive of post bills) of the Bank of Ireland fell from over £3 million on February 1 and June 1, 1819, to £2,751,555 in March 1820. The average circulation of notes and post bills was over £4,400,000 in 1819, was £4,096,296 in the first half of 1820, and £3,838,476 in the second half of 1820.

stated in Parliament in February 1821 that gold was at a discount in terms of Bank of Ireland paper, and that the Bank of Ireland had refused to receive gold on deposit, or to discount bills for merchants who paid their obligations in gold.[1] This touched off a debate on the public responsibilities of the Bank of Ireland, in which Ricardo participated, but led to no action in regard to Bank of Ireland policy.[2]

As a result of the increased gold reserves of the Bank of England and the return of its notes to a par with gold, Parliament authorized the Bank of England to resume payments in gold coin on May 1, 1821.[3] A com-companion law authorized the Bank of Ireland to resume payments on June 1, 1821.[4] Why, when gold was already at a discount in terms of Bank of Ireland notes, Parliament postponed resumption by the Bank of Ireland until a month after resumption by the Bank of England, is not clear. The debate on the bill brought out nothing on the economic issues involved in the resumption of payments, and was in large part simply an occasion for discussing the renewal of the Bank of Ireland charter, which was to come before Parliament shortly.

The resumption of payments by the Bank of Ireland was in effect simply a recognition of an existing situation, and brought no change in the Dublin-London exchange. The rate in London was 9 on June 1, 1821, and between then and October 1822 was never more than $9\frac{1}{2}$ nor less than $8\frac{1}{2}$. The Directors of the Bank of Ireland were, however, concerned over even these moderate exchange fluctuations and the attendant shipments of gold between England and Ireland. On the basis of the report of its Treasury Committee in November 1822, they adopted the resolution:

> "The Bank will, until further notice, take English Bills at par, deducting discount for the number of days such Bills shall have to run. The Bank will, until further notice, pass Bills payable at the Bank of England at thirty days at par; the applicant to pay for the stamp in every case, where the sum shall be under £450 British."[5]

The effect of this action would have been to limit the fluctuation of exchange in Dublin, based on bills payable in London in 30 days, to between about $7\frac{4}{5}$ and $8\frac{1}{3}$. The higher of these rates—the selling rate of London

[1] Presumably this situation continued for some time. On March 19, 1821 a member of the Commons said that gold was at a discount in Ireland (Hansard, Second Series, p. 1336); the London *Times* on August 1, 1821 published an item from the *Hibernian Journal* "that the Bank of Ireland refuses to take guineas in lodgements or payments at the Bank."

[2] Hansard, Second Series, Vol. IV, pp. 339–342. February 2, 1821.

[3] 1 and 2 G. IV, c. 26, May 7, 1821.

[4] 1 and 2 G. IV, c. 27, May 7, 1821.

[5] The text of the Resolution is taken from F. G. Hall, *The Bank of Ireland* (Dublin, 1949), p. 108, whose account is based on the Minute Books of the Bank of Ireland.

exchange—would be in line with the Dublin-London rate of 9½ quoted regularly in London after October 1822. Presumably this was a satisfactory solution, as there was no record of further discussion of the exchange problem by the Directors in the remaining three years of the separate Irish currency.

ASSIMILATION OF IRISH AND ENGLISH CURRENCIES IN 1826

Despite the statement of the Chancellor of The Exchequer, at the time that Sir Henry Parnell had moved for the appointment of a committee to inquire into the assimilation of the Irish and English currencies, that he would support a motion for such a committee at another session, nearly five years passed before a proposal for assimilation was again brought up in Parliament. A plausible explanation of the failure to act on so reasonable a proposal, to which there seemed to be no opposition, was that other Irish problems—bank failures, agricultural distress, and political disorders—were more pressing. Whatever the reason for the delay, there is no record of further Parliamentary action until February 25, 1824. At that time Thomas Wallace, in connection with a notion of Sir John Wrottlesey for the appointment of a committee to investigate a decimal coinage, referred to the Irish coinage and

> "expressed his hope that at some future period the coin of the two countries would be assimilated as well as their affections."[1]

Sir Henry Parnell, that indefatigable supporter of Irish monetary reform, spoke approvingly of Wallace's proposal. Wrottlesey's motion for committee to investigate a decimal coinage was defeated,[2] and neither Parnell nor Wallace pressed for action on the Irish currency.

Over a year later, Wallace, in a carefully prepared statement, in which he reviewed in detail the monetary relations between Ireland and Great Britain and quoted from the Report of the Committee of 1804, moved a series of resolutions for the assimilation of the Irish and British currencies.[3] All who spoke, including the two veterans of the Irish monetary controversy, John Leslie Foster and Sir Henry Parnell, supported the resolutions, and the lack of opposition suggests that the resolutions already had the approval of Government. A Committee, consisting of Charles Rose Ellis, William Wallace, the Chancellor of The Exchequer (Frederick Robinson), and John Leslie Foster was appointed to prepare a bill based on the resolutions. The resulting bill, providing for the adoption of the British currency system in Ireland as of January 6, 1826,

[1] Hansard, Second Series, Vol. X, pp. 448–9, February 25, 1824.

[2] Journal of The House of Commons, Vol. LXXIX, p. 98. February 25, 1824.

[3] Hansard, Second Series, Vol. XIII, pp. 579–582, May 12, 1825.

was considered by the House of Commons in Committee of the Whole, and was passed by both the Commons and the Lords without debate.[1]

The adoption of the exchange stabilization policy of the Bank of Ireland in 1822, and the approval without debate of a unified currency for Ireland and Great Britain were a pale anti-climax to a controversy over Irish monetary policy that had gone on for nearly a quarter of a century. Yet the willingness of the Directors of the Bank of Ireland to adopt a policy of exchange stabilization that their predecessors in office had said was impossible, and the unanimity of opinion with which Parliament approved the assimilation of the currencies, was a full recognition of the principles laid down in the Report of 1804—that the monetary authority in an area can maintain a stable exchange rate through the use of its external reserves and through changes in its credit policy. A few months later, in the hearings before a Parliamentary Committee, two directors of the Bank of Ireland, Arthur Guiness and William Peter Lunell, explained the method used by the Bank to stabilize exchange with London:

> "If the Bank of Ireland requires a supply of gold, in what manner do you procure it?—The Bank of Ireland, in case of requiring a supply of gold, would have to procure it from the Bank of England.
>
> "In point of fact, has the Bank of Ireland within the last four or five months drawn any considerable quantity of gold from the Bank of England?—No, and I will endeavour to state why; the Bank of Ireland has been ready to supply in exchange for its notes bills payable at the Bank of England at twenty-one days date at par, to any required extent, and therefore there was no necessity for procuring a supply of gold.
>
> "Then, in point of fact, you have not created any drain upon England of gold?—Of course we have drawn to a very great extent upon the Bank of England.
>
> "But not directly from coffer to coffer, it was done by giving bills upon the Bank of England?—Yes.
>
> "And you do not know what became of them, or how they were paid? —We have reason to believe they were paid in Bank of England notes, for we issued them in the common and ordinary way of exchange, persons having money to remit to England came to the Bank of Ireland for bills.
>
> "In what mode do you create funds in the Bank of England, in order to meet those bills?—By Exchequer bills, which we thought it prudent to keep for that purpose.

[1] 6 G. IV, c. 79, June 1825.

"So that you create a credit in London available for the purpose?—There are seasons of the year when the exports of Ireland of course are much greater than at other seasons, and the Bank of Ireland is always ready to take good bills on London, or on England payable in London, or payable in Liverpool, at par, charging the interest merely at five per cent upon the period they have to go, which is found to be a great public accommodation, and of course at those periods of the year a large amount in bills is taken and transmitted by the bank, consequently at those seasons we have accumulated an excess of value in London.

"And at other seasons that is run upon by a different state of commercial transactions?—Yes."[1]

For more than a century and a quarter Ireland, as part of the United Kingdom, as a member of the British Commonwealth of Nations, and as an independent Republic, has maintained its currency at par with the British pound through redemption in London exchange and sale of London exchange, in line with the recommendations of the Committee of 1804.

[1] *Report from the Select Committee on Promissory Notes in Scotland and Ireland. Ordered,* by The House of Commons, *to be Printed, 26 May* 1826. Pp. 238–239.

REPORT,

MINUTES OF EVIDENCE, AND APPENDIX,

FROM THE

COMMITTEE

On the Circulating Paper, the Specie, and the Current Coin of IRELAND; And also, on the Exchange between that Part of the United Kingdom and GREAT BRITAIN.

[*May* and *June* 1804.]

Ordered, by The House of Commons, *to be Re-printed,* 26 *May* 1826.

E

THE COMMITTEE, appointed to inquire into the State of IRELAND, as to its CIRCULATING PAPER, its SPECIE, and CURRENT COIN, and the EXCHANGE between that part of the UNITED KINGDOM and GREAT BRITAIN, and to report the same, with their Observations and Opinion thereupon, to The House; and who were empowered to report the MINUTES OF EVIDENCE taken before them from time to time to The House;—HAVE, pursuant to the Order of The House, examined into the Matters to them referred; and have come to the following REPORT:

YOUR Committee having reported to the House from time to time the Evidence and Information laid before them, are now to report such observations and opinions as have occurred on the matters committed to their Inquiry; and they will first proceed on the Exchange between Great Britain and Ireland, which for the clearer arrangement of so intricate a subject, they will consider under the following heads:

1st. As to the Fact of an unfavourable Exchange existing, and to what Extent:

2d. As to the Causes which have created it:

3d. As to the Remedies which can be resorted to for either removing or alleviating the inconveniencies arising from it.

TO elucidate the first point, Tables of the State of Exchange, for a long series of years, between Dublin and London, have been produced by John Puget, Esq. from the books of his house; Accounts have also been obtained of the State of Exchange between Belfast and London, for a few years past, differing from the former, sometimes even so far as 10 per cent; but this difference is fully accounted for. In Belfast the Bills of Exchange are purchased by Guineas, in Dublin by Bank of Ireland and other Bankers' Notes; and if the Exchange between Great Britain and Ireland be stated as it actually exists, where Guineas are the circulating medium, Your Committee would be inclined to think that the Exchange is now and actually has been in favour of Ireland; but if it is to be estimated by the Rates which prevail where Paper is the circulating medium, the Exchange appears to be now, and to have been since 1798, uniformly against Ireland, and to have risen to a degree wholly unprecedented; the former they would call the Real, and the latter the Nominal Rate, and the difference between them arises, as far as Your Committee can form a judgment, from the depreciation of the circulating Paper. They are the more induced to this opinion by observing that the variations in the price of Guineas in Ireland, or, in other words, the Rate of the depreciation of the circulating Paper, keeps pace in general with the difference between this Real and Nominal Exchange. It is true, that some doubts have been entertained whether the price of Guineas has not risen above their intrinsic value in consequence of their scarcity, occasioned, 1st, by the Act imposing a Restriction on their Issue; 2d, by quantities being hoarded; and 3d, by the constant demand for them from the North of Ireland, where the payment of rents, purchase of linen, and almost all money transactions, are carried on chiefly, if not solely, by Specie; but if a person possessed of a Guinea can get for it a Guinea Bank of Ireland Note and also two Shillings, and if the person who wants the Guinea is forced to give in addition to the Bank of Ireland Guinea Note two Shillings to obtain the Gold, it seems evident that the Paper being by so much of less value than the Guinea, is by so much depreciated, more especially when Exchange is the object of Inquiry, which between any two countries is generally, if not always, estimated on the value of Specie or Bullion; and the Guinea in England and in Ireland being the same Coin current in each country, seems to be the true standard to which circulating Paper should be referred for comparison of value. It is not to be supposed, that by any circumstances Guineas can be rendered 10 per cent higher in Ireland than in England, when the expense of conveying them from one country to the other does not amount to 1 per cent; but further, the circulating Paper of Ireland seems equally depreciated when compared with a Bank of England Note; for though a Note of each Bank may profess to represent the same quantity of Gold, the man who wants to obtain the latter will find the former as much inferior in value to it as it is to a Golden Guinea, and he must give the same additional sum to obtain it as to obtain the Guinea. The causes of this depreciation of Irish Paper, and its effects upon Exchange, Your Committee will postpone until they shall enter on the Second Part of the Arrangement they have pointed out: and in proceeding with their Inquiries into the present real state of the Exchange, whether it be unfavourable or not to Ireland, they wish the House to keep distinct in their view the consideration of an Exchange being favourable or otherwise, from that of the degree or rate in which it is so.

Exchange becomes unfavourable to any country when that country, being in debt to another on the whole sum of its money transactions, including all items of Remittance, Balance of Trade, &c. has occasion to transmit more than it is to receive; the expense of transmitting which surplus it must of course defray, and the Exchange is of course against it; this expense (while Guineas can be supplied by the debtor country) ought only to amount to the actual cost and commission on transporting Specie from it to the other, and does not amount to 1 per cent between Dublin and London, including insurance; but any excess in the Rates of Exchange beyond this expense forms a separate consideration, and must arise from other causes, which will be stated hereafter, as far as they have occurred to Your Committee. The inference from this distinction is, that the unfavourable Exchange is generally a symptom of a country having a balance to pay, but the rate of it is not the necessary consequence of that balance, nor does it, or its fluctuations, necessarily or exclusively depend on the amount of it.

The real Exchange, that is, where the Bills of Exchange are paid for in Specie, as in Belfast, having been stated to be in favour of Ireland, during the whole of the year ending 5th January 1803, Your Committee will proceed to examine into the actual state of pecuniary transactions between the two countries during that year (full documents for the last year not having been delivered,) in order to see whether, upon the whole of all accounts for that year, England was to remit a balance to Ireland, or the reverse; and the investigation will satisfy those who think the state of Exchange depends on the balance of Payments, that the rise in the Irish Exchange cannot be accounted for on the principle of that balance.

Appendix, page 153.

Your Committee find by Mr. Puget's Return, that in that year, after paying all Charges and Interest on the public Debt of Ireland, due in London, he remitted to the Irish Treasury the sum of £.1,424,810 on account of the surplus of £.2,000,000 British, borrowed in England, of Money for Lotteries, small re-payments for Seamen, and other articles. They find, also, that the Total Balance of Trade in favour of Ireland, calculated according to the current prices (and they do not think them over estimated) amounted in that year to £.917,299, making together the whole sum to be remitted to Ireland £.2,342,109, against which there is to be set the probable amount of Rents and Income, and other charges for Absentees, about £.2,000,000, to be remitted by Ireland, leaving a clear estimated Balance in favour of Ireland of £.342,109; but if

Appendix, page 185.

Appendix, page 162.

that Balance of trade be computed upon the principle stated by page 107. Mr. Marshall as the proper one, it amounted according to his account to . . . . £.1,816,814

account to	£.1,816,814
instead of	917,299
and the difference	£.899,515

being added, will leave the Balance so estimated in favour of Ireland £.1,241,624. Your Committee are therefore corroborated by these statements in the opinion which they have ventured to offer, that the real Exchange not only was but ought to have been favourable to Ireland; and upon looking forward to the present year, they see every reason to believe that it ought to be still more favourable during the course of it.

They estimate that the Account will stand nearly as follows:

Sums to be remitted from England between 5th January 1804, and 5th Jan. 1805,

On account of a Loan made in England for Ireland, of £.4,500,000 British, of Lotteries, and small Re-payments to the Irish Government . . .	£.5,000,000 Irish.

Sums to be remitted to England for same time,

Interest of the Irish Debt and Charges payable in London, about or rather under . .	£.1,500,000	
For Absentees, about .	2,000,000	
Making together . . .		3,500,000
and leaving a clear Balance of . . .		£.1,500,000

in favour of Ireland against England, exclusive of all considerations of Balance of Trade: But there seems no reason to suppose that the Balance thereof, which was £.917,299 by one calculation, and £.1,816,814 by another estimate in Ireland's favour, in the year stated, should so greatly differ as not only to cease to be favourable in that amount, but to absorb also the other Balance of £.342,109, or of £.1,241,624; by the latter estimate Mr. Coning-
page 58. ham's testimony here has great weight; he thinks "that Ireland has paid every thing she owed, either in her Exports or Bills of Exchange, which she drew on account of those Exports, and that Ireland owes as little upon her Trade now, in proportion to its extent as she has owed at any one period." Your Committee therefore do not hesitate to express their conviction, that the real balance of

pecuniary transactions will be greatly in favour of Ireland this year, and consequently that the real Exchange is and ought to be under Par; of course they feel themselves compelled to seek in other causes than the Balance of Debt for the unfavourable Exchange now subsisting between the two countries; and when they consider the length of time that it has continued, and its progressive rise beyond every thing before experienced, and also that it is un-unfavourable, not to the Debtor but to the Creditor Country, they are led to the conclusion, that the Balance of Debt, so far as it has operated, has tended to lower an Exchange rendered unfavourable to Ireland by other causes.

These causes Your Committee will now proceed to investigate; which leads them to the Second part of their Arrangement, and they will take up the subject from the time of the Restriction Act in 1797.

2.

THIS Act originated in England, from English considerations only; and Your Committee do not mean to inquire into, much less to doubt, the policy or even the necessity of its adoption; they will only observe, that it did not arise in Ireland from any consideration of the circumstances of that country, but was enacted there as a measure supposed necessarily to result from its being enacted in England; they do not find that it was preceded in Ireland by any inquiry into the state of that kingdom; the Exchange was at the time, and had been for a long-continued period before, regularly in its favour; there was of course no reason to apprehend a drain of Specie from thence, and therefore a separate consideration of that country would probably not have suggested or justified the measure; there had not been any alarming demand on the Bank there as in England, nor did the Bank of Ireland apprehend any as the Bank of England did, on the contrary the favourable Exchange was bringing in Specie; and so satisfied were the Directors of the English Bank of there being no apprehension of a drain of Specie from Ireland, that in their evidence before a Committee of the Lords, in 1797, they stated their alarms of a drain from England into Ireland; and their fears even of a Loan being then negociated in England for the use of Ireland are expressed in terms of repeated anxiety. In February 1797, the month when the Restriction was imposed, their Court resolved, "That such a Loan would necessarily endanger the safety of the Bank of England, by the large drains of Cash which it must occasion for the remittance of that sum to Ireland."

Under these circumstances the Restriction passed in Ireland; and to the consequences of it Your Committee must attribute the unfavourable Exchange, and all the high and progressive advances of the Rate.

It compelled the Bank to refrain from sending into circulation, Gold, the only common medium between the Countries—it gave occasion to the great Issue of Paper which followed to replace the Gold so withdrawn, and removed at the same time the best and most effective check against the depreciation of that Paper, namely its convertibility into Gold at the will of the holder—it tended to encourage an unlimited and over-abundant issue, by releasing the Bank from performing their engagements, and by taking away from them the former criterion, namely, the diminution of their Gold, which they were accustomed to look to for judging when their Paper became excessive—it promoted a new and unrestrained trade in Paper Currency, and excited individuals to speculations which interfered with the steady natural Rates of Exchange—the number of speculators so encouraged contributed to raise the price of Bills on England, which being paid for in depreciated Paper the rate of Exchange rose proportionately.

Other evil consequences followed, which tended, in a further degree to assist in depreciating the Paper; forgeries were multiplied, particularly of the smaller Notes substituted for Gold—additional Silver Currency became necessary, and as it was not supplied by the Mint, its place was either filled by small notes, even as low as 6d. without the checks against forgery attending those of larger value; or base coin was fabricated and forced into circulation.

The natural and constant effect of an unfavourable Exchange remedying itself by diminishing the issue of Paper was also counteracted by this measure; for when Exchange is so unfavourable to a country as to draw Gold out of it, it is obvious, that for every Guinea drawn out of the Bank an equal amount of Paper must be drawn out of circulation to be paid for the Guineas; the re-issue of Paper to that amount must be prevented by the decrease of the stock of Specie; the same cause will most probably induce the Directors to diminish their Discounts, so that the quantity of Paper becomes diminished by a still greater amount than the Gold drawn out of the Bank in consequence of the unfavourable Exchange.

Such has been the natural practice of Banks previous to the
page 88. Restriction; Mr. Colville states it in very clear and forcible terms, as

to the Bank of Ireland. Prior to 1797 they limited the amount of their issues as Exchange rose. If prudence had not dictated such a course, necessity would have compelled a diminution of Issues by diminishing the stock of Specie, which could only be replaced at a loss proportionate to the existing rise of Exchange; and Your Committee observe, that in fact as well as in theory, the result of such practice always was and must be the redress of the unfavourable Exchange.

But the Restriction Act freed the Directors of the Bank of Ireland from that necessity, insomuch that Your Committee have to observe, that so far from contracting their Issues in consequence of the unfavourable Exchange, they have increased them, which the state of the Exchange would have prevented them from doing, had there been no Restriction to protect them from the obligation of paying their Notes in Cash.

The fact mentioned by Mr. Colville, of the excessive Issue of Paper in 1753 and 4, and the considerable rise of the Exchange against Ireland which accompanied it, confirms the position, that excessive issues of Paper produce a proportionate rise in the rates of the Exchange; and Your Committee are still further confirmed in this opinion, by observing, that the Exchange immediately became favourable to Ireland, when the failure of the Dublin Banks which ensued, had annihilated the excess of Paper.

The reason is obvious—the nominal Rates of Exchange are influenced by the medium in which the payments are made, and the quantity of that medium necessary to effect a given payment, must be increased as the value of the medium diminishes. This must equally take place, whether the payments are made in a degraded or adulterated Coin, or in a depreciated Paper.

There is a circumstance mentioned by Mr. Marshall, from Doctor Adam Smith, which happened in King William's reign, in the intercourse between London and Holland, which establishes the point, that a depreciated Currency will not fail to affect the Exchange. The British Coin was at that time degraded in England 25 per Cent below its nominal value, and the computed Exchange with Holland was 25 per Cent against England; but on the reformation of the Coin the Exchange fell to Par. If, Paper, therefore, by depreciation comes to represent a less quantity of Money than it professes to do, it must make the Exchange which it is to pay appear unfavourable, in the same manner as Coin in which it were to be paid would have done if by degradation it should cease to contain the same portion of Gold which it used to do; and the removal of the degradation in the one case, and of the depreciation in the other, would have the same effect in bringing the Exchange to Par, or whatever might be its real state.

That this depreciation in Ireland arises almost entirely, if not solely, from an excess of Paper, appears highly probable: and Your Committee, in adverting to the Issues of the Bank of Ireland, do not mean to decide whether the Directors of it might not have had strong reasons for their conduct; but they conceive it their duty to call the attention of the House to a matter of so much importance.

Appendix, (G.) In March 1797, when the Restriction took place, their circulating Paper amounted to between £.600,000 and £.700,000, and on the 1st of January 1804 it was £.2,986,999.

From £.1,000,000 to £.1,200,000 of this increased Paper consisted of Notes of £.1 up to three Guineas, which together with a small part of the issue for larger sums may be considered as chiefly occupying the place of the Guineas withdrawn; so that if the whole of their Paper in circulation in January last be divided into five parts, one will appear necessary as having existed prior to the Restriction; two are to be set down as occupying the place of the Gold withdrawn; and no sufficient reasons have been given for the issue of the remaining two parts, or for the Bank not having diminished its paper, when Exchange rose, in the same manner as they must have done in case the Restriction Act had not been in force. The Issues of the Bank of England afford a very different view. Appendix, No. 13. They were, on the average of three months to 25th March 1797, £.10,431,700, whereof £.268,500 were £.2 and £.1 Notes; and they were, on the 25th of January 1804, £.17,761,090, whereof £.4,711,150 were £.2 and £.1 Notes.

But Your Committee are far from saying that local considerations, and different circumstances at the moment, might not have had a separate influence on the two Banks; they would only add, that Exchange began to rise in 1799, and that the circulation of the page 90. Paper of the Bank of Ireland was, as Mr. Colville states, *concomitant and extended with it;* and that upon comparing the issues of the Bank of Ireland with the rates of Exchange, a strong presumption arises of the connexion between an increased Issue and a high Exchange. For in March 1797. The Paper of the Bank was between . . . . £. 6 & 700,000

And Exchange in Dublin $5\frac{1}{2}$ to $6\frac{3}{4}$:

April 1801. Paper was 2,266,000

Exchange rose from $11\frac{3}{4}$ to 13:

1st January 1804. Paper was 2,986,999

Exchange rose to 17 and 18.

How far the increase of their Paper faciliated or encouraged the increase from private Banks is not clearly established by the evidence; but it appears to Your Committee that the increase of Stamp Duties (even under the observations made by Mr. Beresford) affords some proof of it; and the whole train of evidence respecting country Banks supports the assertion, particularly as to those numerous country Shops throughout the south of Ireland (many of which can hardly be called Banks) who forced their silver notes and I.O.U.'s on the public with such profusion, as, in one instance, not even to have kept an account of them; and the inundation must have been very great, if any inference can be drawn from the number of persons whom the Restriction on Specie encouraged into the business.

On this subject Your Committee deem it necessary to call the attention of The House to the following remarkable facts:

In the year ending 25th March 1800, the number of

Bankers issuing Notes was,	11	
ending 1st January 1801	23	
1802	29	
1803	30	
1804	40	Appendix,

And,

The number of Notes paying Duty in the like periods, was,

	$1\frac{1}{2}d.$	$3d.$	$4d.$	
In 1800	148,112	198,361	104,248	(D.)
1801	245,673	147,211	65,201	(E.)
1802	941,894	196,108	95,600	(F.)
1803	823,673	204,940	67,594	(G.)
1804	1,110,217	256,801	90,265	(H.)

By the existing Law, all Notes under three Guineas may be issued on a $1\frac{1}{2}d.$ Stamp—under £.10 on a *3d.* Stamp—under £.50 on a *4d.* Stamp—whence a judgment may be formed of the increase of Paper Circulation; and Your Committee remark with concern the great inattention which has allowed Silver Notes to get into circulation without having paid the Stamp Duties. The loss of Revenue forms no part of the Inquiry before them; but the omission of the salutary check must have tended to encourage the over-abundant issue which has caused the depreciation of Paper in general, enhancing thereby the price of the necessaries of life, and of all manufactures, encouraging the circulation of base and counterfeited metal, and driving out of circulation what little good Silver had been in it; and above all, keeping up high and unexampled

Rates of Exchange against the Kingdom, unwarranted in their height and continuance by any other great or adequate cause than that depreciation which such an extravagant issue had assisted.

Appendix, (No. 14. (a. b. c.)

It is to be further observed, that very few of those people had registered their firms as by law required; an abstract of which law, as also of the law respecting the issue of small notes, is annexed in the Appendix.

To show the extent of the evil in this respect, which the Restriction promoted, Your Committee have annexed the best account they could procure of the number of Banks, and other houses, which have been invited by it to partake in the profit of issuing Notes and Tokens, amounting to above 200, but probably to a much larger number now; and they have added the detailed account of one district, to show the quality and low condition of the generality of the people who were thus encouraged to overwhelm an unfortunate country with their Paper.

Appendix, (N.)

Mr. Beresford, in his evidence, expresses his opinion, that the number of new country Bankers, who have started up since the Restriction, has made the Circulation of country Paper at least four times what it was.

Your Committee have not sufficient grounds to form any correct opinion as to the present amount of Issue by private Dublin Bankers. Mr. Colville seems to think the issue of all private Banks in Dublin and the country equal to that of the Bank of Ireland. Mr. Beresford does not think the issue of those in Dublin exceeds £.700,000. The practice of some of the great Army Agents in depositing with their private Bankers in Dublin, the Notes which they received from the Bank of Ireland, for payment of troops in the country, and sending in their place the Notes or Post-Bills of such Bankers, justly met the disapprobation of Government, and orders have been issued very lately for checking it. In further support of Mr. Colville's opinion, it must be also observed, that as the Restriction has made it necessary for every private Bank to keep a stock of Bank of Ireland Paper, equal, or nearly so, to what it would have otherwise deemed prudent to keep in Specie for paying its Notes, the facility of procuring that stock is increased by the increase of its quantity in the market; and although such part of that Paper as is employed in forming that stock may be said for the time to be locked up from circulation, yet it must be remembered, that all such stock gives room to and necessarily implies an issue of the private Banks Paper equal not only to it but to such further amount as Bankers in general may in prudence suffer their outstanding Notes to exceed their stock of Specie lying in their coffers.

Other causes might be assigned to support the supposition of there being too great an issue of Paper in Ireland; such as, the increased facility of borrowing on Discount—the practice of long Discounts out of all established mercantile course, mentioned by page 111. Mr. Frank; but Your Committee deem it unnecessary to adduce them, being clearly of opinion, that the high Exchange is in itself a sufficient presumptive proof of a depreciation of Paper, and that this depreciation is in itself also a strong presumptive proof of an over quantity of Paper being in Circulation.

Your Committee will therefore proceed to the smaller subordinate matters which have affected the rates, and particularly promoted the frequent fluctuations, of Exchange.

The first which attracts their attention is the mode adopted for bringing to Ireland the surplus of the money borrowed in England for the Irish Government, which is minutely detailed in the evidence of Mr. Puget and Mr. Crofton.

Your Committee do not mean to impute any blame to the conduct of the Irish Treasury, on the contrary, the directions given by the Commissioners thereof seem to have arisen from a just anxiety for the public benefit; but the nature and constitution of their office appears to be unfitted for executing the business of Exchange and Brokerage beneficially, even if their proper duties allowed them leisure for the purpose, and if the Law, commonly called the Responsibility Act, under which they are appointed, and the Address of the House of Commons to His Majesty on the Institution of the Bank, detailed in Mr. Crofton's examination, prescribed their undertaking it. Mr. Crofton shows that they did not enter upon the management of the receipt of that money as an object of Finance; he states their universal object to have been the regulating and steadying the Exchange, rather than deriving any great profits to the Exchequer; but their interference appears to have rendered it unsteady, and to have created fluctuations, even to 4 per cent—their Drafts have been sold on 'Change at advanced prices—their regulations as to the amount or minimum of each Draft, left all persons wanting to remit any sum under £.1,000 at first, and afterwards under £.500, out of the range of being accommodated at the Treasury, and to buy at advanced prices from those who had got Drafts there—their endeavours to prevent partiality or preference seem to have been ineffectual; it is true, a book was ordered to be kept to take down the names of persons applying, but the sums applied for were not entered; and although Mr. Crofton says such a book could be produced, Your Committee cannot avoid observing, that the Paper returned to their order does not purport to be a book or copy of a book, the entries in it begin only on 6th September 1803, and end on 14th November 1803, all written apparently at one time, and in one hand.

The number of days sight at which the Drafts were drawn varied from 3 to 21 days; for which variations sufficient motives have not been laid before Your Committee.

Mr. Roach gives his opinion, "that the system of the Treasury drawing on England has been prejudicial to the Exchange; and if any other mode could be adopted, it would have been better, he means, drawing by the Treasury at all. The system has held out some temptations to jobbing; numbers of people calling at the Treasury for Bills, while they drew, and retaining those Bills to job with afterwards, when the Treasury did not draw; the Exchange, generally, when the Treasury stopt drawing, rises in a much greater proportion than it otherwise might; and that there has been much fluctuation in Exchange since the practice of the Treasury drawing commenced." This rise, which has gone in a few days even up to 4 per cent, is effected by those dealers in Ex-
page 113. change whom Mr. Frank considers as Speculators, "who make large purchases at the Treasury when they are drawing, with a view to sell again at a considerable advanced price on 'Change;" whose intervention is no way useful, and who necessarily create an artificial rate of Exchange highly injurious.

page 126. Mr. Puget's observation is very strong "that any attempt on the part of the Treasury to lower Exchange must necessarily prove either disadvantageous or abortive, particularly the latter, as Government can only draw as their occasions require, and their Funds in England will permit;" and respecting their power of preventing fluctuations, his words are, "that when the amount of Drafts drawn by the Treasury, and the short periods they were drawn in, is considered, to any impartial commercial man, knowing the Dublin Market, it will appear astonishing that the fluctuation was so little." Mr. Colville "does not hesitate, to say that some regulations are necessary in order to put the drawings under a proper management;" and it is worthy of observation, that although the
page 118. Appendix, No. 15. Treasury drew upon London between the 3d March and 3d April 1804, for £.585,960, yet the Exchange was not reduced lower than to 16½, and that only for 17 days of the month.

Your Committee now proceed to the 3d and most important head of their Arrangement, the Remedies of the Evil; but first they wish to observe upon an opinion entertained by some of the witnesses, that the present high Exchange operates as a tax upon Absentees, and is in effect a bounty on export, and a discouragement to import. If the real Exchange were unfavourable to Ireland the opinion might have some foundation; but if it be, as it has been already suggested, in favour of Ireland, the Absentee who receives his Rents in Guineas has a gain instead of a loss on the remittance; a fact which is felt and acknowledged by all proprietors in those districts where rents are so paid. On the other hand, if the rates of the nominal Exchange against Ireland arise from the depreciation of the circulating Paper there, that depreciation must equally affect the resident and the absent proprietor; the difference is, that the Absentee sees the depreciation reduced to an item in his account, when the Paper is to be converted for him into the Currency of another country, but it operates on the Resident, by raising the price of every thing, and though he feels the effect, yet its operation is so blended with the price that it does not present itself ostensibly.

As to an exchange founded on depreciation operating on exports **page 62.** and imports, Your Committee cannot express their sentiments in clearer terms than Mr. Borrowes uses, when he says "that such an Exchange has not the smallest influence on the Trade of the Country, either by encouraging its exports or checking its imports, because in the case of exports the exporting merchants pay as much more as the depreciation for every article which the exporting merchants draw back in the Exchange; and which renders the Exchange nugatory upon Exports; and in case of Imports, the importing merchants receive so much more as the depreciation amounts to, which prevents Irish Exchange acting as a restraint, and thereby an exchange founded on a depreciated currency, stands upon principles totally different from an Exchange founded on a currency not depreciated."

3.

THE great and effectual remedy to the high and fluctuating Rates of the Exchange, undoubtedly, would be the Repeal of the Restriction Act from whence all the evils have flowed; the common circulating medium being thereby restored, the rise of Exchange above Par would be limited to the expense of transporting Specie, and Paper being convertible into Gold its depreciation would be prevented. The expense and difficulty to which the Bank of Ireland

and other Banks might be exposed, in the event of the Restriction being taken off, under the present circumstances of the Exchange, form however a strong argument against the sudden adoption of such a measure.

No other reason arising from commercial motives has suggested itself to Your Committee for its continuance in Ireland, more especially if the real Exchange be favourable, as they have already stated that it must be in their opinion; but as its continuance may be connected with political considerations, the discussion of which would involve Your Committee in a very extended and tedious Inquiry, they abstain from entering into the general expediency of removing or continuing the Restriction at the present time, or into any conjecture of the period when it may be expedient.

Such remedies, therefore, as may answer to give redress during its continuance, are next to be considered; and the great object of many of those which have been suggested, is the procuring a common circulating medium in the absence of Guineas.

With this view, a consolidation of the two Banks of England and Ireland has been proposed and supported with very plausible arguments by Mr. Borrowes; but its expediency seems rather problematical; and when the rapid advances which the Manufactures, Trade, and Agriculture of Ireland have made since the establishment of the Bank, and the great assistance which they have received from it, under the wise and liberal conduct of its Directors, are considered, Your Committee cannot recommend the putting those benefits to a hazard, even if the redress of a high Exchange could be ensured thereby: but, putting the hazard out of the question, the measure seems impracticable without the consent of both Banks, which the evidence shows very unlikely to be procured.

Other modes of obtaining a common medium, such as that of inducing or even compelling the Bank of Ireland to give Bank of England Notes in exchange for their own on demand, or to make their own exchangeable for them in London, or to give Bills of Exchange on London for them, have been suggested; and there is no doubt any of them would have the effect of rectifying the Exchange. The objection that has been made to this proposal, is the difficulty and expense to the Bank of Ireland which would attend the procuring a Fund in London on which to draw. On this Your Committee observe, generally, that neither the difficulty nor the expense attendant on this measure would be so great as that to which the Bank, by its constitution, is necessarily subject at all times when not protected by a restriction from performing its engagements; and that whatever funds the Bank formerly applied, or intend again to apply, on the removal of the Restriction, to provide for the difficulty and expense of obtaining a supply of Gold, might in the interim be applied to the procuring of English Bank Notes; the evidence of Mr. Winthrop points out the practicability of obtaining a sufficient supply of Bank of England Notes with such a fund; his expression is, that "the Bank of Ireland, or any person, may procure Bank Notes now to any extent if they will pay for them." But Mr. Mansfield's evidence so clearly shows the practical mode of carrying this measure into effect, that Your Committee cannot impress it too strongly upon the attention of the House; it shows, in the example of Scotland, how effectually a very small sum, vigorously and wisely applied, did operate, and that Banks there did establish an adequate fund with ultimate advantage to themselves.

His Account states, that "there was, after the Peace of Versailles in 1763, an Exchange of 5 or 6 per cent against Scotland with London, created by persons collecting Gold from the different Banks there, bringing it to London, and passing their Bills at Edinburgh for it, in order to put a profit into their own pockets by raising the Exchange. The two chartered Banks of Scotland, seeing that this Exchange arose from artificial means, collected as much funds as they could to bring to London, and by drawing gradually at ½ or 1 per cent less than the others, reduced the Exchange to what they esteemed Par Bills of 40 days date;"—at which it has steadily continued ever since, unaffected by the failure of the Bank of Ayr; the convulsions to credit in general in 1792 and 1793; the failures in 1795; and the difficulties which caused the Restriction in 1797 in England, but which was not extended to the chartered Banks of Scotland; and all this notwithstanding the great presumption, that if an account of all pecuniary transactions between Scotland and England could be ascertained, it must have often happened that the balance was against the one country or the other.

This fact gives great force to the arguments of those witnesses who propose that the Bank of Ireland should establish a credit for the like purpose in London; and the present peculiar situation of the Irish Finances not only points out a ready, but an adequate and effective fund, which at the same time that it gives to the Bank of Ireland every prospect of success which has attended the measures of the chartered Banks of Scotland, exempts it from all expense, risk or difficulty which might attend it; for Your Committee must observe, that the Bank of Scotland undertook to provide this Fund at their own expense, but the Bank of Ireland has an opportunity of establishing it without expense to themselves; and further, it appears to have been suggested to the Banks of Scotland by their good sense and patriotism, to try the efficacy of a measure without precedent, while the Bank of Ireland has only to follow an example where success has been already demonstrated by experience.

Your Committee has stated, that the great Loan, and other smaller sums to be remitted this year from England to the Irish Government, amounts to £.5,000,000 Irish; they have also shown that there is reason to believe the mode used by the Irish Treasury of bringing over the Loans from England has been prejudicial to the Exchange; and the whole weight of evidence goes to show it could be much more advantageously managed by the Bank of Ireland; they therefore recommend that immediate measures should be taken with the Bank of Ireland for the purpose, and for their establishing an effectual fund in London for drawing on, whereby they may gradually reduce the Exchange in the manner somewhat resembling that which was adopted by the Edinburgh Banks. If any argument should be thought necessary in aid of the strong practical example which Scotland affords, they would refer to the
page 123. evidence of Mr. D'Olier, and of others, but particularly Mr. Irving,
page 61. who states, "that if the Bank were to invest part of its capital in England, thereby furnishing a fund which would at all times give it the means of drawing, it would in such case have a control over Exchange operations, of such power as to enable it at all times to regulate the Exchange;" and he says again, "that he would consider
page 62. a Loan of 2, 3, or £.4,000,000 in England for the use of the Government of Ireland, paid into the Bank of England, to be placed there to the credit of the Bank of Ireland, to operate to all intents and purposes as such Fund." Mr. Irving adds, "that the creation of such a Fund in London might, and most probably would, be attended with considerable expense to the Bank, but the evil of the expense would be temporary, the good would be permanent to the Bank and to the public." This plan, he says, "would necessarily oblige the Bank of Ireland to be dealers in Exchange, which would be a new source of advantage that would more than compensate the additional risk and trouble." And Your Committee are inclined to think that the Union measure makes it expedient that they should deal so now, whatever might have been their interest or practice before; and that it is the duty of both Banks to endeavour, to the utmost of their power, to render the money dealings between the two countries as free from fluctuation, and at as steady

a Par at all times as it is between Edinburgh or Liverpool and London; and they agree entirely with that gentleman in his opinion, "That a Bank, having an exclusive charter, exacts from its directors a two-fold duty, a duty to the proprietors and a duty to the public, which, operating together, would make the directors avoid sacrificing their duty towards the public to the interest of the proprietors." In this case however the interest of the proprietors of the Bank of Ireland and the Public seems to be the same; and there possibly and probably is another fund, which that joint interest might induce the directors to invest in the Bank of England, or use for the benefit of the Exchange, if they were legally empowered, namely, whatever surplus they have of Specie in their coffers, over and above what they are allowed by law to issue, or what a due consideration of the circumstances of Ireland might show it prudent or necessary for them to keep there. Of the amount of such surplus Your Committee do not pretend to form any judgment; be it what it may, it is as useless both to the Bank and to the Public where it lies as if it were buried by them in the earth; but by being applied to free Exchange from the mischiefs which oppress it, it might be of essential service. If an unfavourable Exchange should even take the whole of such surplus out of the country, which is by no means to be supposed, a favourable Exchange, which would be the probable consequence, must soon bring it back again, and mean time it would not only operate beneficially, but might have the advantage of being at least as completely secured for the Irish Bank proprietors as it is now.

Another means of aiding the endeavours of the Bank in creating such a fund of credit in London occurs—the vesting the Government with power to issue Treasury Bills to the Bank, not to be made use of unless they should be found necessary to support that credit; and another and effectual resource still remains—their enlarging their Capital for the purpose; so that upon the whole of the Government Loans in England; the redundant Specie now locked up, the contingent aid of Treasury Bills, and a power to the Bank of enlarging its Capital; Your Committee cannot entertain a doubt of the practicability of what they recommend, nor that it ought to have the sure effect of reducing Exchange to par. In case of such event they would also strongly urge the doing away the name of Exchange, and putting an end to its calculation, by equalizing the Monies of Account and Monies of Circulation in both countries, and the fixing the future interchange by Bills at a stated number of days, adequate to defray the expense of remitting at all times, so as fully to adopt the same practice which prevails between Edinburgh and London, and between Liverpool and London. In mentioning Liverpool (which is divided from Dublin only by the page 65. intervention of the Irish Channel) it is worthy of remark that Mr. Irving states "the separation of Ireland from Great Britain by the sea not to be an obstacle to the fixing an invariable Exchange between Dublin and London, because it seldom happens the variation page 55. of posts exceeds many days:" and Mr. Mansfield's evidence deserves again to be recurred to, when he says, "that no inconvenience of any kind had resulted to Scotland from the system, except the temporary one of the Banks having to provide funds in London at the commencement of it; on the contrary he asserts it was productive of the greatest good."

But all the benefits proposed by this mode of remedies would be of little avail, and of very limited duration, if it did not promise at the same time to cure the depreciation of Paper in Ireland by diminishing its over issue; a consequence which Your Committee are firmly persuaded must follow, the Bank of Ireland Notes being made convertible into Bank of England Notes, almost in the same manner as if the Restriction ceased, and they were convertible into Gold; for if the fund in London of the Irish Bank should be too rapidly drawn on at any time, they must limit their issue of Notes to lessen the demand on that fund, their Notes would of course lose their depreciation, and become of equal value with the English Notes, into which they would be convertible, or in other words with Guineas, while English Notes shall be undepreciated; and Your Committee do in express terms declare their clear opinion, that it is incumbent on the Directors of the Bank of Ireland, and their indispensible duty, to limit their Paper at all times of an unfavourable Exchange during the continuance of the Restriction, exactly on the same principle as they would and must have done in case the Restriction did not exist; and that all the evils of a high and fluctuating Exchange must be imputable to them if they fail to do so. Your Committee have a proof of the effect which rendering Bank of England Notes procurable in Ireland would have upon the Exchange by the great fall of it from Dublin on London, in the months of March, April and May 1797, when Government passed Bank of England Notes in Dublin; and this further benefit will attend the reduction of the quantity of their Paper, that it will Appendix, page 131. operate as a preparative for more speedily removing the restriction on the Bank whenever other circumstances shall allow the measure to take place. Your Committee however do not wish to be understood as recommending the reduction of the Paper of the Bank of Ireland otherwise than cautiously and gradually.

It may be material also to assist their endeavours by a diminution of the Issue of Paper from private Bankers and other dealers; to effect which much attention should be given to restrain the Paper of the country Banks, by a strict enforcement of the laws respecting the Registry of Bankers, and the full payment of Stamp Duties. It will also deserve consideration whether at a future time all Bankers whatever, except the Bank of Ireland, should not be prevented from issuing any Notes or Post Bills under £.10 or 10 Guineas, as Mr. Roach mentions; and as soon as a proper and suffi- page 82. cient Silver Currency is procured, it would seem expedient that the issue of Silver Notes should be entirely suppressed.

Before Your Committee quit the subject of Exchange they wish to observe, that if their inquiries have failed in enabling them to propose any effectual remedy, still a remedy ought to be sought for by the wisdom of the House; for that a great country, now placed as Ireland is under the same Legislature with England, forming a constituent part of the United Empire equally as England, or any county in England does, its metropolis not so distant from London as any part of Scotland, Newcastle, Carlisle or Durham, should labour in its pecuniary intercourse with England under a constant varying Exchange which the others are free from; that the intervention of a narrow sea, with regular daily packets and speedy means of mutual transport, should cause an encumbrance in the mutual Interchange of Money, which does not exist where the distance by land is greater, and the communication by Post not more frequent, nor more expeditious; that there should be no Exchange, or an Exchange commuted for a regular number of days between Edinburgh and Liverpool, and Bristol with London; and that an Exchange must exist, or is incapable of such commutation between Ireland and London; and that the evils which this long Inquiry have investigated should be entirely without remedy, are positions so strange, that Your Committee cannot believe them to be founded in the common nature of things, and must impute to their own insufficient investigation, or want of sagacity, the not having pointed out an adequate remedy, if they have failed to do so. They will only add, with respect to the money drawn from Ireland, that remittances to Absentees did exist before the Restriction to a considerable extent, without producing an Exchange constantly unfavourable; and that if the high rates of Exchange really operate as a tax on them, it does not appear politic or reasonable to continue any such tax with a view to encumber the resort of any Irish subject to the seat of Government, and to the deposit of his dernier resort of justice, more than that of any inhabitant of Scotland, or any county of England; and when it is considered, that, if in the natural order of things, undisturbed by such a measure as the Restriction on Specie, the remittances to Absentees, by causing a balance of pecuniary intercourse against Ireland, would force an export from thence wherewith to pay it, and restore the level, it may be fairly concluded, that the Absentees, by bringing over their money to England, force the manufacture or produce to follow them, which, but for their coming, they would necessarily have caused to be used at home; the only difference is, that the produce or manufactures which their incomes naturally promote would come to be consumed or used in England, in the stead of being consumed or used in Ireland; and thus the encouragement to the productive industry of Ireland may be said to operate in both cases, though certainly the non-residence of men of fortune on their estates, is in many respects a great and lamentable misfortune to the country.—On the other side of the account, with regard to the temporary influx of money to Ireland, from Loans for Ireland in England, the temporary remittance of which has been said to operate as a set-off against the drain of the Absentees, much as they may occasionally tend towards rendering the Balance, and of course the Exchange, favourable, Your Committee cannot recommend them as desirable on that account. It should be remembered, that the relief they afford is temporary, while the drain of interest and charges, which they create, is permanent, and that the advantages which the great Loan of this year must produce to the Exchange, by its transmission, ought not to supersede resorting also to a diminution of Paper, as a means of permanently rectifying the Exchange. Their injurious effects go still farther: each Loan, by supplying a means of paying any balance of debt due to England, interrupts the natural effect of that debt, to force out export and check import, so as to allow the Money Accounts to right themselves, and produce the proper level; it also, by the same operation, encourages import, in providing a ready fund wherewith to pay for it; and it will appear from the papers before Your Committee, that the imports of Ireland increased during the last five years, (in each of which a considerable Loan was made) compared with the Appendix, No. 12 five preceding years, at the average rate of £.1,422,000 the year, and the exports decreased during the same time, on a like average, in the sum of £.239,000 official value; while the average annual remittances for the Loans, including some small payments by Mr. Puget, during those last five years, was £.1,406,000. Your Committee feel with satisfaction that this view of the injurious effects of the Loans from England tends to dispel the gloomy prospect of the distressing and still more increased height of Exchange, when public circumstances shall allow the system of Ireland's raising the larger portion of her annual Supply by such Loans to be altered, the suppression of this system will then naturally tend to make her increase her exports and diminish her imports, and bring Exchange to Par.

THE Specie and current Coin of Ireland remain to be considered. The Evidence very fully points out the miserable situation of the Silver Coinage, or rather of the base metal and notes and I.O.U.'s. substituted in its place.

This evil is clearly to be traced to the unfavourable Exchange. The state of the Exchange naturally caused the Silver Currency of Ireland, so long as it was degraded only in the same degree with the Silver Currency of England, to transfer itself to this country, where it would pass for the same sum as English Silver Money. The place of the Irish Silver Coin so withdrawn was supplied in many parts of Ireland by Silver Notes; but in Dublin, where Notes of a very small description are not issuable, by an extremely base Silver Coin, which was privately fabricated in great quantities, and to which nothing but the want of any other medium capable of effecting small payments could have given Currency. Some im- page 73.
pediment having arisen to the circulation of the very base Silver, the attention both of the Bank of Ireland and of the Government was called to this subject, and measures appear to have been taken in consequence of a communication with His Majesty's Privy Council for the Coinage and Issue, by the Bank of Ireland, of a considerable quantity of Dollars, at the price of six Shillings Irish per Dollar. These Irish Dollars contain the same quantity of Silver with those lately issued by the Bank of England at five Shillings British, and differ little in appearance, except in having the name and device of the Bank of Ireland in the place of those of the Bank of England.

Your Committee think it proper to call the attention of the House to the difference in value between the two kinds of Silver

Currency thus introduced into the two countries. The Dollar of the Bank of England is very nearly equal in value to the 5*s.* for which it passes; the Dollar of the Bank of Ireland, if the Exchange were at Par, would be nearly equal in value to 5*s.* 5*d.* Irish. The additional 7*d.* for which it is made to pass, is a further and a nominal value, which it is obvious that it has been found necessary to give to it, in order thereby to secure the continuance of its circulation in Ireland, under the present circumstances of the Exchange; for if it had been exchangeable for 5*s.* 5*d.* of the present Irish Paper, there would have been a profit on the exportation of it. Your Committee lament the necessity which has thus arisen for suffering the state of the Exchange, even in any case, to prescribe the value which shall be given to the current Money instead of providing that the value of the current Money shall limit, as it ought ever to do, the fluctuations of the rate of Exchange.

It is to be observed, however, that the measure of issuing the Silver Currency in question, at the price of six Shillings, is not the Act of Government; that the Irish Dollars are not the legal or standard Coin of the kingdom, being deemed to be a mere token, the name Token being inscribed upon them; that they are not Cash within the meaning of the Act of Parliament imposing the Restriction; and above all, that they are resorted to only as a temporary expedient.

Your Committee have been led to enter into these particulars by a wish to point out the temptation to increase the nominal value of the current Coin to which a country is subjected under the present circumstances of Ireland, and also by an anxiety to assert the principle, that no depreciation, either of the chief or even of the inferior Coins of these kingdoms, ought to be looked forward to as the means of remedying the evils resulting from a too extensive Issue of Paper, and from a consequently unfavourable Exchange; and they cannot conclude this branch of their subject without remarking that the state of the Silver Coinage of Ireland, and the circumstances which have attended it, form an additional argument in favour of those measures for rectifying and fixing the Exchange which they have recommended in the preceding part of this Report.

When the Exchange shall be reduced to its proper state, it appears to Your Committee that the 6*s.* Dollar ought to be called in at the expense of the Bank of Ireland.

The supply of Silver, which it is in contemplation to procure, consisting of Dollars only, without smaller change, is very short of the quantity supposed to be necessary; and the present distresses from want of Silver all over Ireland, if suffered to increase, or even continue, must add to the depreciation of Paper by increasing the quantity in the worst shapes, through the medium of small Bankers, and Shop-keepers with very inadequate capitals; on this subject it may be proper to remark, that the laws against the issuing of counterfeit or base Coin, as well as against the forging of Bankers Notes, requires to be amended and carried into more strict execution.

The Copper Coinage is so defective that it appears there is not a Mint half-penny in circulation; and if it shall be thought expedient to equalize the Currency, by making the Shillings contain only 12*d.* Your Committee submit the advantage of doing so, if it could be accomplished with due regard to other circumstances, before a new Copper Coinage shall take place; and the making a Copper Penny, Halfpenny, and Farthing of England, equally current in Ireland as the Silver Shilling or Golden Guinea; and to abstain from coining any Copper with any separate device, or under any separate weight or description for Ireland.

Your Committee have annexed to this Report such further Papers and Abstracts as they have received, for the better information of The House. Forming the 4th part of the Appendix.

May and *June*,
1804.

SELECTIONS FROM MINUTES OF EVIDENCE

EVIDENCE OF JAMES MANSFIELD

Banker in Edinburgh

of the Firm of Mansfield, Ramsey and Company

March 8, 1804. Pp. 32–33, 54–55

Is there any Exchange between London and Edinburgh?—There has been for these last 25 years to my recollection, by drawing at 40 days.

How much per cent do you estimate that to be?—The drawing at 40 days I estimate at ½ per cent, or a little more.

Who pays for the Stamp?—The person who demands the Bill.

If a person having money in London wants to draw upon his correspondent, what premium has he for giving a Bill either to the Banks of Scotland, or the private Bankers there?—He can pass his Bills at 20 days, or at ¼ per cent; the Bank or Bankers not paying for the Stamp, the drawer pays it.

Do you recollect any period when the Exchange was otherwise?—I do not recollect it; but I have heard it was after the Peace of Versailles; it was then at or about an Exchange of 5 or 6 per cent; the cause of it arose, as I understand, from artificial means, by people collecting Gold from the different Banks, bringing it to London, and passing their Bills at Edinburgh for the same.

What was the object of carrying the Gold to London?—To raise the par of Exchange, and to put a profit into their own pockets by so doing.

How long did that last?—I cannot say how long, but for some considerable time; it began to alter some time about the year 1770; the two chartered Banks of Scotland seeing that this Exchange arose from artificial means, began to think of collecting as much funds as they could bring to London of their own; those funds they lodged partly with the Bank of England, and partly with their own Bankers, and the Banks then began to reduce the par rate of Exchange gradually, by beginning at to perhaps ½ per cent or 1 per cent less in drawing on London till they reduced it to what it has been since.

How did they replace this money that they drew for?—By getting all the manufacturers Bills which they must draw upon the correspondents in London for goods; also Army Bills, and Bills for gentlemen of fortune who had money in England.

Why were those Bills sold to the Banks in preference to others?—Because from the capital of the Banks they were enabled to get money from no where else; the other Bankers not being able to purchase them because they could not sell them again for a profit.

What was the nature of the currency of Scotland at that time?—The general circulation was Paper; at that time one of the Banks put into their Notes an optional clause of paying them 6 months after sight; but I shall be able to give better information as to dates and circumstances on some subsequent day.

Did the convulsion which happened in 1792 or 1793 to credit in general, produce any effects on the Exchange of Scotland?—It did not alter it in the smallest degree, nor did it when the restriction on the Bank of England took place in 1797.

Was there much distress felt in Scotland to the mercantile transactions during those two periods?—Very great in both, by the stoppage of the trade of all manufacturers.

Were there many mercantile failures?—There were a great many, and would have been a great many more if the Exchequer Bills had not been issued in 1793.

Were great sums applied for and granted?—A good deal, especially at Glasgow.

Was the quantity of Bank and Bankers Notes in circulation at that time considerably diminished?—Those of the public Banks were not diminished at all; but the private Banks, from the pressure of the times, were obliged to diminish them greatly, and some of the private Banks were obliged to stop payment, and some never resumed it; the public Banks rather augmented their accommodation to the country.

At what period was the confidence and the circulation of the private Banks restored; and what was the state of the circulation in 1795?—Soon after the issue of Exchequer Bills took place confidence began to be restored; but the circulation was greater prior to the stoppages of 1792 than it came to be in 1795.

How was the comparative circulation, when the restriction of the Bank took place in 1797, with 1795?—The difference was very small; I speak as to the Bank of Scotland, of which I am a Director, not of the circulation in general; I think the circulation of the Bank of Scotland gives a criterion by which to judge of the general circulation of Scotland.

How is it at the present time compared with 1797?—It is less at present than it was 18 Months ago, but I am not at present enabled to state with respect to 1794.

. . . .

In what manner are the balances of the different Banking houses adjusted in Scotland?—They must either pay in Specie or Bank of

England Notes, or give Bills on their correspondents in London, at the par rate of 20 days.

Is there any period at which such mode of adjustment took place in your recollection?—It has been as long as I remember.

When ready money in Edinburgh is paid for a Bill, payable at 20 days date on London, does not the remitter pay an Exchange on his Bill equal to the value of the interest for 20 days on the sum remitted?—Yes, because the par between Edinburgh and London is at 40 days.

When a bill is drawn at 40 days, does not the remitter pay a higher Exchange than when drawn at 20?—Certainly not, otherwise than that there is a difference in the interest between the 20 days and the 40.

Why do you call 40 days the par?—Because we have found from experience, that it has answered the intercourse between Edinburgh and London.

In estimating the interest on a Bill of Exchange payable in London, should it be calculated by the remitter at 5 per cent, or at the medium rate of mercantile profit?—I calculate it at 5 per cent.

Does not a Bill or Draft drawn in Edinburgh on London at sight, bear a premium?—It certainly does; a premium of 20 days, or about ¼ per cent.

Do you consider the 20 or 40 days interest to be a compensation in the nature of commission, for the trouble attendant on the transaction, rather than as any proof that the Exchange between the two is not at par?—I decline answering the question, as being a matter of opinion.

Are you of opinion, there is any Exchange between London and Edinburgh?—I refer to my former answer.

Are you of opinion, there is a balance of trade, and remittances against Scotland with England?—Yes, I should think so.

Whether such a state of things would not create an Exchange unfavourable to Scotland?—I apprehend, that a mutual communication of trade may exist between the two countries, without creating any Exchange at all.

Do you not mean that the difference between the exports and the imports which it is necessary to pay for, may be discharged by the means of temporary advances by the Banks or mercantile houses of one country to the Banks or mercantile houses of the other country?—Certainly; and I look upon the establishment of the two chartered Banks in Scotland to be of great use and importance in this point.

When Bills at 20 days are taken in discharge of balances from one Bank to another, is there any and what allowance made to the Bank receiving such Bills in payment?—None; these Bills are taken at par as Specie.

Is it not the present custom of the Edinburgh Banks to give Bills on London at a fixed date for their own Notes offered for payment in Edinburgh?—Yes.

Was it not the custom, antecedently to 1761 or 1762, for the Edinburgh Banks to give Bills on London at a rate which was not fixed for their own Notes offered in payment in Edinburgh; that is to say, at a rate depending on the fluctuation of the Exchange?—Yes, I have always understood they gave Bills on London at a rate according to what they understood to be the existing rate of Exchange.

When the fluctuating Exchange, which you have stated to have existed before 1761 or 1762, was put an end to by the introduction of the custom of the Banks giving Bills on London at a fixed date, do you understand that all the Banks, public and private, at once came to an agreement to make this change in their system of drawing?—I cannot speak as to the private Banks; but the chartered Banks understood one another, and the rest were obliged to follow.

How many private Banks are there in Edinburgh?—I cannot tell.

Did the change operate materially to the inconvenience or prejudice of the private Banks?—I apprehend not; but on the contrary, for their good, as the country benefited by the measure.

Has the Exchange continued steady since that time?—It has never varied at all.

Whether any great demands for Bills on London from the Edinburgh Banks were made at the time of that change, and in consequence of it?—There was a great demand at first, but gradually decreased as the Exchange was reduced.

Were those demands made on all the Banks, or the public Banks alone?—Principally on the public Banks.

Did the public Banks increase their capital at that time?—No, but they called in that part of their capital which had not been paid up, to the amount of £.10,000 Sterling.

Do you know the amount of the Paper circulation of Scotland, previous to this change?—I do not.

Do you not conceive that the change of the system which took place, had the effect of diminishing, in some degree, the quantity of paper circulation which had existed immediately before?—I certainly do think so, as I have already stated; it was in consequence of there being more Paper in circulation than the situation of the country required.

Do you conceive that the augmentation of Paper which had taken place prior to the change of system, had resulted from a too great extension of the Paper of the old Banks, public and private, or from the issue of the Paper of Banks recently instituted?—From both.

Had the unfavourable state of Exchange commenced nearly at the time when these extraordinary credits were given, and the new banks were instituted?—Much about that time.

Was the over issue of Paper prior to the unfavourable state of Exchange, or subsequent?—Certainly was prior, as it was the cause of the system being altered, which remedied the rate of Exchange; and I certainly think that the over issue of Paper was the cause of the high rate of Exchange.

Do you conceive that since the change of the system, the balances of the Cash accounts kept by the Edinburgh Banks with their correspondents in London have been more fluctuating than before?—I do not conceive they have been more fluctuating, excepting in times of public mercantile calamity, such as in 1792 and 1797.

Do you then mean, that in the case of a fixed Exchange it is necessary for the Edinburgh Banks to possess larger funds in London, as a provision against any distressed state of credit in Scotland, than it would be necessary to keep if there were a fluctuating Exchange, as there was at the period antecedent to 1763?—No; when Exchange is fixed I do not apprehend it is necessary to have more funds in London than when it was in a fluctuating state.

Has any inconvenience of any kind resulted from the change of the system, except the temporary one of the Banks having to provide funds in London at the commencement of it?—On the contrary, it has been productive of the greatest good.

How long was it before the Exchange was brought to a fixed rate? —It was done gradually, in the course of about two or three years.

EVIDENCE OF ROBERT BARNEWALL

Merchant in London

March 16, 1804. Pp. 50–51

Do you not conceive that an augmentation of the circulating medium of Ireland necessarily tends to the augmentation of the nominal price of commodities?—I believe so.

Is not the nominal price of commodities in Ireland at this time, that is to say, the price of commodities, as compared with Irish Bank Paper, higher than the nominal price of commodities in Great Britain, that is to say, of commodities in exchange for English Bank Paper?—I do not know.

Must it not necessarily be the case, since there is a difference of about £.10 per cent in the Exchange?—I apprehend that a man in Ireland holding an English Bank Note must submit to nearly the loss in the Exchange that he would be negotiating a Bill, the Bank Note being payable at sight, may be negotiable at ½ per cent higher than a Bill that is payable at 31 days.

Cannot the owner of a Bank of England Note for £.100 buy with it more goods in England than the owner of a Bank Note in Ireland can buy in Ireland with a Bank Note of Ireland amounting to £.108. 6*s*. 8*d*. which is the par of Exchange?—I cannot answer.

Supposing a man to be able to buy the same quantity of goods in England for £.100 English, which he can buy in Ireland for £.108. 6*s*. 8*d*. Irish, must there not be an extra profit of 10 per cent on the exportation of British goods to Ireland, inasmuch as the proprietor of £.100 English Bank Note, can buy with that Note a Bill for about £.118 in Ireland?—There is no doubt but the importer of English goods in Ireland must increase his price in proportion to the rate of Exchange at which he pays for them.

Do you then consider the 10 per cent rise, which has lately existed in the Exchange between England and Ireland, an indication that there may have been a general augmentation in the nominal price of commodities in Ireland of about 10 per cent?—I conceive there must, on commodities imported from England.

May it not be presumed that there must have been the same rise on all that class of commodities which are exported from Ireland to England, inasmuch as there must otherwise have been an extra gain of 10 per cent on such exportation?—It seems probable there must be a proportionable rise on the goods exported from Ireland.

If it is presumable that there has been a rise equal to the rise in Exchange in the Irish price of all goods exported both from England to Ireland, and from Ireland to England, may it not also be presumed that there has been nearly a similar rise on articles produced in Ireland, and used for home consumption?—I think not.

Do you not think there must have been such a rise, if by the term rise is meant a higher price than would have subsisted if there had been no augmentation of paper, and no rise in the Exchange?—I am unable to answer that question; but, on reflection, with respect to goods exported to England from Ireland, I apprehend the exporter may sell the goods exported at a lower price in England, on account of the high Exchange he obtains for his Bill, than he would if he negotiated it at a more moderate one.

Supposing, as you conjectured to be the case, that the price of Irish goods is raised in the Irish market by the augmentation of paper, will there not be a new temptation to import from England the kind of goods which are so raised in Ireland, and will there not be a new obstruction to the exportation of the goods which are so raised in Ireland, which will lead to an augmentation of the imports into Ireland, and to a diminution of its exports, supposing the Exchange to remain as before?—I feel myself incompetent to answer the question.

Must not an augmentation in the Irish price of corn, for example, as exchanged for Irish paper, produce a disposition to import corn from England, supposing the Exchange to remain the same as it was before the rise?—I conceive so, if the Exchange remained at par.

Must not the same augmentation in the Irish prices produce an indisposition to export Irish articles, supposing the Exchange to remain the same as before?—No doubt; as gain is the object of every man, either in exporting or importing, if the object is taken away, the practice would not be continued.

Must not such disposition to import, and indisposition to export, supposing it to be followed by actual increase of imports, and an actual decrease in exports, produce what is commonly called an unfavourable balance of trade, and must it not lead to the creation of a greater number of English drawers of Bills upon Ireland than there are of English remitters?—If the imports are increased, and the exports diminished, no doubt it must produce an unfavourable balance; there cannot be a greater amount of Bills drawn than there are remitters to take.

Will not such disproportion between the amount of Bills which there is a disposition to draw, and the amount of Bills which there is a disposition to remit, produce a rise in the Exchange with Ireland?—If the Bills to be drawn exceed the money to be remitted, the Exchange naturally will rise.

Will not that rise in the Exchange operate as such a bounty on the exports from Ireland, and as such a tax upon the imports, as to counteract the high price of Irish goods in Ireland which the excessive issue of Paper in Ireland has been supposed to have created?—A rise in the Exchange above what it is now or has been, would tend to reduce the intercourse between the two countries, rather than to operate as a bounty.

Must it not, in proportion to its magnitude, operate as a bounty on exports, and as a tax on imports?—It must; in the manufactures exported from Ireland there are a number of foreign materials, which it would operate as a tax on.

Supposing this bounty on exports, and tax on imports, to be exactly countervailed by the rise in the price of commodities in Ireland, will not the relative situation of Ireland, with respect to its trade with other countries, remain exactly the same?—I do not know that; there would be a greater capital necessarily employed.

Will not the capital be the same, if computed in foreign money, though it would be greater in Irish money, if computed according to the price of currency in Ireland?—I apprehend not. I am giving conclusions upon matters which I do not feel myself competent to.

Would not therefore the reduction of the quantity of Paper in Ireland be the means of improving the state of the Exchange?—If the Bank were to diminish their discounts, people would be obliged to draw on this country for money, which they can now obtain without doing so, and the Exchange would probably decline.

EVIDENCE OF JOHN IRVING

Merchant of London

March 20, 1804. Pp. 59–60

Have there been great fluctuations in the Exchange?—There have.

Have those fluctuations been caused by any circumstances not immediately affecting trade?—I think the high Exchange has been occasioned by other causes than those affecting trade; but the fluctuation, I think, has principally arisen from the greater or less demand for Bills.

Is there any particular cause which will occasion that demand to be more at one season than the other?—I think there is, particularly in that season when Money is demanded, in order to supply the purchasers of salted provisions; the linen markets at specific periods; and those periods when it is known that the Treasury must draw upon England.

Suppose the Treasury left the power of drawing to the Bank of Ireland upon the Bank of England at their discretion, would that fluctuation be any way likely to be remedied thereby?—I think a fund being invested in London, upon which the Bank of Ireland might at all times have it in their power to operate, would give them the ability of correcting fluctuations of Exchange.

Explain what fund should be invested, and how it should be provided? —The fund which would be the most convenient to invest, I should consider to be the Government securities of England, bearing interest, which at all times might be converted into Cash according to the demand, such as Exchequer Bills; I take it for granted that there is a fund in England to be remitted to Ireland, which, in place of remitting, I would invest in the manner before stated.

Do you mean, that the Loans should be first invested in Stock or Exchequer Bills, to be converted into Cash from time to time, and if so, explain how that differs with respect to the effects on the Exchange, from the Loans being remitted or drawn for as heretofore, and at present? —The spirit of my reply to the questions put to me, why there would be less fluctuation in the Exchange between Dublin and London, by a public fund being in the direction of the Bank in place of the Treasury, is this; that the periods of drawing by the Treasury are known; the Bank, by having it in their power to be always drawers of Bills, would give a supply according to the demand, and therefore there would never be too large a quantity of Bills at Market.

Do you think that the Bank drawing Bills for smaller Sums than it is in the habit of the Treasury to draw, might not likewise tend to prevent in a greater degree that fluctuation complained of?—I think it would be a point of convenience, but would produce no real effect on the Exchange.

Do not you think that if the Treasury draws for low Sums under £.1,000, and that the persons who want Bills for a smaller amount, go to a person who has got the £.1,000 draft, he does not pay a higher rate of Exchange, than what such person paid to the Treasury?—I have never known in the course of my experience, any difference of price betwixt a Bill of large amount and one of small; I speak of London, being ignorant of the fact as to Dublin.

Do you not think that the directors of the Bank of Ireland, as dealers in Exchange, would feel it their duty to that body whose trustees they are, to take the best profit they could make, unless they were restricted by Government in respect of their agency for Government?—A Bank having an exclusive charter, I am of opinion, exacts from its directors a two-fold duty; a duty to the proprietors and a duty to the public, which operating together, I think would make the directors avoid sacrificing their duty to the public to the interest of the proprietors.

Do you admit that these two duties are in opposition to each other? —I do not; but I do say that they are inseparable.

EVIDENCE OF WILLIAM COLVILLE

Merchant and Director of the Bank of Ireland

April 14 and 17, 1804. Pp. 88–90, 97–98

Was it the practice of the Bank, antecedently to the restriction, in any degree to restrain the total amount of its loans, when it experienced a diminution of its cash in consequence of an unfavourable Exchange, or of any other circumstances producing a drain of its Guineas?—It must be very obvious, that if the directors of the Bank did not pay a very great attention to such an important consideration, they would be very unfit to conduct the business put under their care.

Do you then mean to say, that they were accustomed to lessen the total amount of their loans, including loans in the way of discounts, when they found their Guineas going from them?—I certainly do.

Did not that limitation of loans necessarily operate as a limitation also of the total amount of their circulating Paper to an equal amount?—It certainly does generally, but from the nature of the case, it is impossible to state the specific proportion.

Would not the Bank Paper in such case be necessarily reduced, not only in the degree in which the loans were reduced, but even in a still greater degree, namely, in the same proportion also as the Gold of the Bank was diminished?—It certainly would; and, in the former answer given, I think I have explained it.

Suppose, for the sake of illustration, the Bank loans to have been £.500,000, and its Notes £.500,000, and its Gold in its coffers to have been also £.500,000; and suppose also, that, in consequence of a drain produced by an unfavourable Exchange, £.50,000 of its Gold should be withdrawn; suppose also, that, in consequence of this drain, the Bank should reduce its loan £.50,000, is it not presumable that its Notes would be reduced to £.400,000; £.50,000 of its Notes being reduced in consequence of the reduction of loan, and £.50,000 in Notes being brought in in payment of the £.50,000 in Money which had been taken out?— . . . It certainly would.

Do you then admit, that, antecedently to the restriction the Paper of the Bank of Ireland naturally diminished itself whenever Gold was drawn out of the coffers of the Bank, supposing even its loans to remain the same?—As the Notes came in for the payment of Cash, the Cash was diminished, and the circulation of Paper was diminished in the same proportion; but in all those cases, the prudence of the Bank induced them to call in their loans, in order to strengthen the Bank provisionally against the continuance of such a drain.

Was there not then a two-fold cause of the limitation of Bank Paper when the Exchange was unfavourable; the one, the natural limitation just mentioned which took place through the cancelling of the Notes brought in for Cash which was demanded, and exported; the other, the limitation of Paper produced through the reduction of the loans of the Bank of Ireland?—To give an answer to that, as a general principle, I must say, that whenever drains of that kind are made either upon a public or a private Bank, prudence directs that the extent of the circulation of Paper should be lessened by every means in the power of that Bank; first, by cancelling those notes which are paid in Specie; and secondly, by calling in loans to lessen the circulation by that channel also. I give this answer as to the general principle; but here I will point to the particular fact. The reason of the calls upon the Bank at that time, just before the restriction Bill took place, did not arise from a high Exchange against the country, but from the political situation of the country itself, which was at that time under the pressure of an incipient rebellion, it being about one year before the time it actually broke out.

In what manner do you conceive that the limitation of loans operates in lessening a drain upon the Bank for Guineas?—Suppose that all the loans of the Bank amounted to £.500,000, and that the Bank called in those loans, and that it is the practice of the Bank to receive nothing in payment but their own Notes, it clearly follows, that £.500,000 of Notes being taken in in that channel, does as effectually cancel them as if they had come in at the counter, and been discharged in Specie.

Supposing the drain upon the Bank for Guineas to result from a very unfavourable Exchange, which should make it profitable to export Guineas, and supposing the case which you have put, namely, that of a limitation of loans, and a consequent limitation of Notes, to the extent of £.500 000, would not the drain upon the Bank still continue in case the Exchange should remain the same; and would not the opportunity of exhausting the Gold of the Bank be still afforded to the holders of any Notes remaining in circulation, as well as to any persons having a right to draw upon the Bank of Ireland; and would not therefore the limitation of loans be ineffectual to its purpose, except so far as it might have the effect of improving the Exchange?—The answer to this question is very important, because it will develop the reasons upon which the restrictions of the two public Banks have not only been laid on, but the necessity of the policy being still continued, particularly in Ireland, as long as the course of Exchange is above par, and decidedly against that country. In order to explain that further, suppose the restriction Bill to cease, the Bank must then proceed to pay off all Cash Notes whatever, and that is to be done by calling in as much of their loans as they find is necessary, in order to leave no more Notes in circulation than what the Cash in the Bank is able completely to cover.

Were not the directors accustomed, antecedently to the restriction, to limit their Paper, as a means of lessening the drain of Guineas occasioned by an unfavourable Exchange?—I believe I gave an answer before in the affirmative.

Could such reduction of Paper have lessened the drain of Guineas if it had not improved the Exchange?—As far as the Guineas so drawn out went to pay the balance against the country, so far they operated to the reduction of the Exchange against the country, by paying off so much of its debt, and so far only.

If the Guineas only operated by paying the debt, why was there any necessity for limiting the Paper in the manner you have stated that the directors were accustomed to limit it?—The way I answer that, is this; It is blending two views of the subject together, which cannot, in my humble opinion, be understood without considering them separately; namely, one of the views applies to the conduct of the Bank, which must be directed by its relations; the other is a general subject, that, in my humble opinion, does no longer bear upon the Bank than the moment their Notes are in and the Cash is out.

Supposing a suspension of Cash payments to take place, and the Exchange to become unfavourable, but no Gold to go abroad, and to become the means of improving the Exchange, do you conceive the limitation of loans, as a means of limiting Bank Paper, is likely to have any influence in lowering the Exchange?—I do not exactly know whether the answer I shall now give to that question will be satisfactory, but this seems to me to be a proper time to remove what, I apprehend, has been a very great error in judging of this difficult subject; namely, it has been generally thought that the extension of Paper in Ireland has been a cause of raising the Exchange, but my opinion is directly the reverse, inasmuch that as far as the circulation of Paper has supplied the circulating medium, it enabled the Gold which before stood in its place to be exported out of the country, and, as far as it went in weight and measure so far it was a clear and decided cause of preventing the Exchange from getting to a higher pitch than it has hitherto attained; but to go to a further answer to that part of the question, which relates to the extending or lessening the loans of the Bank, in this view of the subject, it must be evident that the more Paper issued by the Bank in consequence of an extension of loans, that so far as it extends the Notes of the Bank it further enables a greater drain of Specie to take place, and consequently, to strengthen the cause which keeps down the rate of Exchange.

If antecedently to the restriction the Bank in point of fact was used to limit its Paper in the event of a very unfavourable Exchange, and if antecedently to that period, the Exchange in point of fact never was more than from 1 to 2 per cent against Ireland; if on the other hand, since the restriction, the Bank in point of fact has suffered its Paper to enlarge itself under the circumstance of an unfavourable Exchange, and if that unfavourable Exchange has become as much above par as 10 per cent against Ireland, is there not a presumption, arising from experience, that a limitation and not an enlargement of Paper is the means of lowering the Exchange?—The answer to this question, will, in my humble opinion, explain another error, and not a trifling one indeed, in which I think this question is involved. The high Exchange in Ireland has not altogether been concomitant in point of time with the restriction Bill, inasmuch as it appears to be the fact that 2½ years passed over in which Exchange not only vibrated about par, but the extraordinary instance existed where the Bank Paper of England was sold upon the Exchange of Dublin at 3⅓ per cent under par, and I wish the particular attention of the Committee to this singular fact, as it will lead to clear inferences that will not only explain that the word depreciation, as it relates to the subject of Paper, is not a positive but entirely a relative term, which I shall take the liberty of explaining in other parts of this subject, when I shall be questioned thereto. As far as my answer goes coupled with parts of my evidence before this day, it must appear that my opinion is, that the circulation of Bank Paper in Ireland is in no shape the cause of the high Exchange; and it therefore seems incumbent upon me to point out what is the real and efficient cause, which is, that Ireland owes more Money than she is able to pay.

When you state that the high Exchange was not altogether concomitant with the restriction Bill, do you mean to imply that it was not concomitant, or nearly concomitant, with the augmentation of Bank Paper?—I believe the fact to be this; the restriction Bill took place in March 1797; from that period to 1799 there was a considerable increase of Bank Paper, yet Exchange not only vibrated about par, but in an instance I have stated, was considerably under it. After 1799 Exchange began to rise, and the circulation of Paper was concomitant and extended; but as we can account for that high Exchange clearly and decidedly, I am not inclined to resort to causes that are entirely problematical, and, in my mind, do not bear upon the subject at all; or if they do, have a very contrary tendency to the effect attributed by others.

Did not that considerable increase of Bank Paper, which you state to have taken place till 1799, consist chiefly in an augmentation of small Notes which were not in circulation antecedently to the restriction?—I have no Paper at present by me to enable me to answer that question accurately.

. . . .

Do you then admit that a general augmentation of the circulating medium of a country, whether consisting of Gold only, or of Gold and Paper, or of Paper only, has a tendency to augment the price of articles in exchange for such circulating medium?—It certainly has, unless as the circulating medium augments, that the articles are to be influenced by it do not augment in an equal proportion.

Supposing the circulating medium to consist, as is now the case in Ireland, of Paper exclusively, or almost so; and suppose such Paper to be augmented in quantity; suppose also the general price of articles in exchange for such Paper to be raised, as you have admitted, will not such rise operate as a temptation to foreign countries to enlarge their export of Goods into Ireland, as long as the Exchange shall remain the same; inasmuch as an advanced piece of Goods in Ireland, other things being equal, must give an additional profit to the foreign exporting merchant?—I think, before this question can be answered, the state of Exchange, which is mentioned in the question, must be more particularly explained, that is, whether the Exchange is against the country or in favour of it; but as a general principle, I have no objection to give it as my opinion, that the raising of the price of a foreign commodity in any country, higher than what it was before, must be an inducement to bring in more of those goods into that country.

Will not the same general advance of prices in Ireland, which an augmentation of Paper is admitted to produce, operate as a discouragement to the exportation of Irish articles, as long as the Exchange shall remain the same, which shall be assumed to be at par?—I can give no answer to this; but again repeat, that, as a general principle, every thing that raises the price of the article to be exported, so far as that raised price goes, operates to lessen the exportation of such commodities.

Will not this augmentation of imports into Ireland, and diminution of exports, occasion an increase of Drafts upon Ireland, and a diminution of remittances to Ireland, and a consequent rise of the Exchange?—I certainly think that whatever increases the imports, and decreases the exports, must tend to put that country in a worse situation than it was before, and consequently to raise the Exchange against it.

Do you not then admit that an augmentation of Paper in Ireland, since it has a necessary tendency to raise the price of goods, and since the rise in price of goods has a necessary tendency to augment the imports into Ireland and to diminish the exports, and since that augmentation of imports and diminution of exports of necessity raises the Exchange, may be considered as the radical and primary cause of a rise in the Exchange?—I think, as a general principle, that an undue issue of Paper will operate in part to the end mentioned; yet, with the permission of the Committee, I will beg leave to put them in mind of Mr. Hume's opinion on this point: Mr. Hume, who certainly was the greatest writer on those subjects, in my humble opinion, was a decided enemy to Paper circulation; and he argued, upon the principles which we have now been considering, that every increase of the circulating medium, whether of Gold or of Paper, that bore upon prices and raised them, tended to increase imports and to decrease exports; but if I recollect him right, he said, and made a strong distinction between the increase of Gold and the increase of Paper, inasmuch as the increase of Gold was the object of every nation's attainment; and that the bad consequences from such increase of Gold was only those evils which necessarily attended all human affairs whatever.

If an augmentation of Paper has (as you seem to admit) a tendency to raise the Exchange in the manner which has been suggested, does it not follow that such rise in the Exchange will be proportionate, or nearly so, to the augmentation of the price of commodities in Ireland; and will not the rise of Exchange form a compensation to the merchant exporting goods from Ireland for the too high price to which goods in Ireland have been raised?—I should be sorry if it was understood that the circulation of Paper is the cause of the high Exchange; it has been induced by political necessity, and if the Restriction Bill is continued, it must be continued from the same cause; for, upon reference to a former part of my evidence, it will be found, that I gave an express opinion, that as far as the circulation of Paper went in Ireland it had the effect of keeping down the Exchange, and not of raising it; the high Exchange against Ireland being clearly and decidedly to be accounted for independent of the circulation of Paper at all.

EVIDENCE OF JEREMIAH D'OLIER

Director of the Bank of Ireland

April 17, May 2 and 8, 1804. Pp. 91, 116, 123.

At what rate of interest has the Bank of Ireland been used to lend to Government?—5 per cent.

What rate of interest do you conceive the Government funds to have afforded to the holder during the last year?—About 5½ per cent, I believe.

At what rate have you lent to individuals?—5 per cent.

At what rate do you understand that Bankers have lent to their customers, and what rate of interest have Merchants allowed in account to persons having cash lying with them?—The legal interest in Ireland is 6 per cent; the Bank is restricted to 5 by law; private Bankers in Dublin, I believe, have charged 6 per cent but I am not certain they do now; but there are Gentlemen here present who can fully answer that question.

Is it not evidently the interest, both of the Government and individuals, to borrow indefinitely of the Bank at 5 per cent?—I wish the word indefinitely to be explained.

Would it not, for example, be the interest of the Government, instead of raising a loan at about 5½ per cent for the services of the year, to borrow the whole of the sum wanted at 5 per cent and may it not be presumed that the Government would prefer resorting to such a measure as a means of economizing the public Money, unless, proceeding on political principles, they should refrain from doing it on the grounds that such a mode of raising the supply would lead to too great an extension of Bank of Ireland Paper?—The answer to that is, that it is clearly the interest of the borrower to raise Money on the lowest terms possible, and equally the interest of the Bank of Ireland to lend its Money only upon such conditions, that the repayments are practicable by the borrower both in point of time and amount, suitable to the convenience and the wants of the Bank; and therefore no loan can be proposed by any minister to the Bank which shall be presumable not to be payable within a very limited time, and to a very limited amount, as he must be subject at all times to the demands and necessities of the Bank, who are the lenders. The Bank of Ireland was instituted for commercial purposes, and must at all times have in view the accommodation of the commerce and manufactures of the country, and they are besides restrained by law in the manner of their lending to Government.

Would not such a loan to Government as has been supposed, be deemed by the directors objectionable on the grounds of its tending too much to increase the quantity of Bank of Ireland Notes?—The Bank of Ireland at all times was particularly careful to restrain their loans upon that kind of security to such an amount as perfectly satisfied themselves that the extent of their Paper in circulation should by no possibility affect its credit.

Is there not nearly a similar interest in private Individuals to borrow indefinitely at 5 per cent on the credit either of Stocks, or of Bills of Exchange?—If by the term indefinite, I am to understand loans without limitation as to their amount, I must answer, that whatever may be the advantage proposed by those to themselves who become applicants for such loans, that by the principles and conduct of the Bank they would be refused, and restrained to what would appear to be the necessary demands for their trade.

[Here follows the passage quoted on page 41]

. . . .

Would not a reduction of Bank of Ireland Paper have a tendency to diminish the sum total of the Paper of Ireland?—I believe not.

Do you mean then that the sum of Bank of Ireland Paper which should be withdrawn would be exactly replaced by the Paper of the private Banks?—I believe it must.

Do you conceive that every augmentation of Bank of Ireland Paper causes a proportionate diminution of the Paper of private Banks?—In some degree it certainly does; but the introduction of the representation of Silver by Paper, has, in my opinion, greatly increased that kind of representation beyond the wants and the convenience, as well as the safety of its payments, and of course by so much as the amount of that Paper there is a new circulation, and of course a very considerable increase of Paper Money.

Do you conceive, that every augmentation of Bank of Ireland Paper produces an exactly proportionate diminution of private Bank Paper, and that every diminution of Bank of Ireland paper produces an exactly proportionate augmentation of private Bank Paper, supposing all other circumstances in the country to remain the same?—The general effect will be, that by so much as Bank of Ireland Paper is withdrawn, its place will be supplied by private Bankers Paper, and so *vice versâ*.

When the Bank of Ireland, antecedently to the restriction, reduced its loans and consequently its Paper, as it was the custom to do on the occasion of a very unfavourable Exchange, do you conceive that such limitation of Paper produced an exactly proportionate augmentation of the Paper of private Banks?—Certainly not; but it left distresses incalculable upon the merchants and traders, who wanted aid, which they could not obtain either from the public Bank or the private Banks.

Did not the same circumstances of a drain for Guineas, which led to the limitation of the loan of the Bank of Ireland, operate in the same manner in restraining the loans, and consequently also the issues of Paper of private Bankers?—Certainly it did.

Supposing the Bank of Ireland now to diminish its Paper, would not the increased difficulty of obtaining that Paper operate, in some measure, in the same manner as a difficulty in obtaining Guineas operated in restraining the disposition to lend in the private Banks?—I think not in any degree whatever.

Suppose the private Banks in Dublin which issue Paper were to give Bills on London at a fixed Exchange for such portion of their Paper as the holders of it requested to have so exchanged, following in this respect the same practice with the Bank of Ireland, and refraining from the re-issue of the Paper which would be so exchanged, do you not conceive that the general Paper of Ireland would then necessarily be reduced nearly in the same proportion?—It appears to me that the Dublin Bankers would speedily get rid of their trade and the transaction altogether.

. . . .

Are you of opinion that a Loan of £.2,000,000, £.3,000,000, or £ 4,000,000 in England, for the use of the Government of Ireland, to be drawn for by or remitted to the Bank of Ireland, as the Bank in its discretion should direct, would operate as such a fund as Mr. Irving recommends, for the purpose of keeping down and steadying the Exchange?—So far as the sum mentioned will amount to or exceed the payments to be made by Ireland to England, and for its other foreign engagements, it will certainly operate to lower the Exchange, perhaps to par, and if the excess be considerable, to below par.

Do you not imagine that that fund would operate more effectually under the management of a commercial house, like the Bank, than in the manner hitherto practised by the Treasury?—Wherever it is conducted on mercantile principles there will be no question that the rate of Exchange will be regular, and all violent fluctuations avoided; I do not presume to put any censure upon the manner in which it has hitherto been conducted at the Treasury, but I am to suppose the persons there were governed in their conduct by orders, or from some principles of which I am not acquainted.

Do not you imagine that by its being conducted on mercantile principles by the Bank of Ireland, improper speculations may be prevented, and a knowledge of the times when Money is to be drawn, and of the quantity to be drawn, would be more effectually prevented, so as to save those fluctuations which such knowledge creates?—I believe it probable.

Do not you think it would?—I do, and I think it ought to do so.

Describe the inconveniences in the manner of the Treasury's drawing, as it respected the Exchange?—I conceived there was a general apprehension that the high price of Exchange was not any thing less than a combination by interested individuals; the fact was, that the high price of Exchange was the true price according to the mercantile interests of the country, and that any attempt to lower it below such price, was, in its effect, as far as related to the drawing by the Treasury, a loss to the Public, though there was no other intention than that of giving a general accommodation of what appeared to those officers the fit and proper rate at which those Bills drawn should be sold; but it had frequently happened that when the Treasury had finished their drawings, that the Public, not being sufficiently supplied with Bills, the Exchange advanced, as I have described, from 1 to 2 per cent and perhaps sometimes upwards.

EVIDENCE OF ROBERT MARSHALL

Inspector General of Imports and Exports of Ireland

April 20 and 24, 1804. Pp. 101–103, 106–107

Are you of opinion that the Paper currency of Ireland at large is depreciated?—I am clearly of that opinion, for the reasons I have mentioned.

To what causes do you ascribe the depreciation of Paper, whether from discredit, or over issue, or otherwise?—As to discredit, I never heard the solvency of the Bank of Ireland doubted by any one, and I am inclined to impute it to an over issue, but I cannot give a decided opinion; I mean an over issue of Paper in general, and not of the Bank of Ireland particularly.

Do you conceive there could be an over issue of Paper in general, if there was not an over issue from the Bank of Ireland?—I should think it possible. I do not think there is any effectual check or limitation to the issues of the private Bankers. I cannot conceive that they often experience a run in consequence of any alarms in the country, because their Paper is in general considered as good in the event of any disturbances in the country, as the Paper of the Bank of Ireland.

Do you not conceive that the limitation of the Bank of Ireland Paper may have a tendency, in some measure, to limit the Paper of the private Banks?—I apprehend so to a certain extent.

Do not you conceive that the difficulty of detection of forged Bank of Ireland Notes by the holders of them in the country, has a tendency to prevent their circulating there to the same extent as the Bank Notes of the country Bankers in the immediate vicinage?—I am inclined to answer in the affirmative, but I have never lived in the country parts of Ireland.

State your opinion as to the Exchange?—The rate of Exchange in general, properly speaking, may be defined to be the difference between the quantity of Bullion paid for a Bill in one place and received for it in another. 2dly, In places where Specie is of the same weight and purity (as in Dublin and London, for instance) the real rate of Exchange is the difference between the quantity of such Specie paid for a Bill in either place, and received for it in the other. 3dly, In order to find the real rate of Exchange between one place and another, the currency of the two places must be reduced to some measure of value common to both. 4thly, Ireland exchanges with London only, and she exchanges, generally speaking, through Dublin. 5thly, The real rate of Exchange therefore in

Dublin, results from the existing state of the entire pecuniary intercourse of Ireland with all countries. In Dublin, Bills purchased with Specie, or, which is the same thing, with Bank of Ireland Notes, equal in amount to Specie, at their market price, have generally yielded in London more Specie than they cost in Dublin, ever since the suspension of cash payments, except during the two years of scarcity in 1799 and 1800; with the exception of these two years therefore, the real rate of Exchange has been generally in favour of Dublin. That the Exchange has appeared to be against Dublin is owing to its being always computed in Bank Notes, which having ceased to represent the full quantity of Specie for which they were issued, require an additional number of them to make up that quantity; this additional number has swelled the Exchange, and made it appear to be against Dublin, when in reality it was in its favour.

A state of things somewhat similar has often occurred, and particularly during the reign of King William, in the intercourse between London and Holland. Dr. Adam Smith mentions, that the computed Exchange with Holland was then, owing to the clipt and debased state of our Coin, 25 per cent against London, though the real Exchange might have been in its favour; the Exchange, no doubt, was computed in the depreciated currency of the day, as the Exchange in Dublin is at present.

We may at any time form a pretty good idea of the real rate of Exchange between Dublin and London, by the rate between Belfast and London, as these two rates have never been known to differ more than from ½ to 1 per cent, unless affected for a moment by some special circumstance. They are alike at present, the difference being only in the manner of expressing them; were they both expressed in Bank of Ireland Notes, or in Specie, they would be found to be about £.16. 10*s*. in the one case, and £.6. 10*s*. in the other, in both places; the rate of Belfast therefore having been generally in its favour of late years would be another proof, if it were wanting, that a favourable rate has also existed in Dublin during the same period. However difficult it may be to persuade our Absentees of the fact, it is nevertheless true, that with regard to the Exchange they are gainers by residing out of the country; were they in Ireland they would receive indeed about 10 per cent more than they receive at present, but then their receipts would be in Bank Notes, which will not go so far in purchasing any commodities as Specie by 10 per cent. If they were to convert these Notes into Guineas, and with the Guineas to buy Bills upon London, which they may do either in Dublin or Belfast, at about £.106. 10*s*. such Bills would yield £.1. 16*s*. 8*d*. more in London than they would pay for them in Ireland; and I know not how it can be proved, that the rate as now quoted of £.116. 10*s*. is in favour of our export merchants. I am well aware that they are benefited by what is usually called an unfavourable Exchange, but the Exchange is a favourable one, and therefore disadvantageous to them; for instance, suppose an exporting merchant should send to London a certain quantity of linen to the value of £.100. British, and having then a credit in London to that amount, he should go upon 'Change in Dublin and sell his Bill for it, he will certainly sell his Bill for £.116. 10*s.* but he is paid in Paper money, which will yield only £.106. 10*s.* Irish currency, just £.1. 16*s.* 8*d.* less than he had in London. Now an unfavourable Exchange was always known to produce to the exporting merchant more Specie in Dublin than he had credit for in London, as every exporting merchant will recollect to have been the case whenever he sold his Bill above par, prior to the depreciation of Bank of Ireland Notes.

If we take a general view of the circumstances which have principally caused the exchange to be favourable to Ireland, notwithstanding the additional drains occasioned by the Rebellion and by the Union, we shall find those circumstances to be, 1st, The large remittances from the British Treasury, for such part of the English Loans as were not retained for Interest. 2ndly, The money which, since the Union, we have ceased to send out of the country for the pay of the six regiments on foreign service. These sums have amounted upon an average of the six years, ending 5th January 1803, to about £.1,400,000 per annum, a sum which has not only counteracted those additional drains, but must have left so large a surplus to be added to the excess of our exports over our imports, as to have greatly improved the annual balances of debt upon our entire pecuniary intercourse with Great Britain, and from this improved state of those balances has resulted the favourable Exchange above mentioned. In the early part of last year I made out a statement—(See Appendix, No. 11)—of the balances of debt, as well as I was able, for every year since the suspension of Cash payments; and from the correspondence which in general exists between the respective balances and the real rate of Exchange, it may be fair to infer that the statement has sufficient relative accuracy. Upon examining the balances in this statement, in order to see whether they have had any influence upon the depreciation of Bank Notes, it appeared that the balance of the year 1797, when the depreciation began, was the most favourable ever known in Ireland, owing not only to a large excess of our exports over our imports but to great remittances from the British Treasury; and it should also be reremarked of this year, that it was preceded by an Exchange steadily favourable to Dublin, which proves that we did not owe a balance to London; the depreciation nevertheless originated in this year, and at one period of it was upwards of 3 per cent in Dublin, and about 5 per cent in the North. Afterwards, during the two years of scarcity, when the balances were really unfavourable, the depreciation did not exceed 3 per cent.

And since, though the balances have been always favourable, the depreciation has risen to 10 or 12 per cent. From this examination we may conclude, that the depreciation has not been influenced by the state of the balances of our external transactions, and that no excess of our exports over our imports, nor any favourable balance of the entire pecuniary intercourse between the two countries, that can reasonably be expected, will have the effect of raising Bank Notes to the value for which they were issued. I will now endeavour to trace the progress of the depreciation, through the various events which may be supposed to have led to the hoarding of Specie, in order to see how far the depreciation is to be attributed to circumstances connected with the security of Ireland. Prior to the Rebellion of 1798, the depreciation was not much more at any time in Dublin than 2½ or 3 per cent. About the time of that Rebellion, the depreciation rose to about 5 per cent; it was soon reduced in the North, and at times became scarcely perceptible, in consequence of some judicious arrangements made by Government for supplying the demands of the military. From the suppression of the Rebellion to the end of the war with France, the depreciation fluctuated from 15*s.* to 5 per cent. From the Preliminaries to the King's Message, which may be considered as a period of peace, the depreciation gradually fell to 2½, and then rose in like manner to 4½ per cent. From the recommencement of the war till a few days prior to the insurrection on the 23d of July last, the rise was not very material; but just about the period of that event there was a sudden rise to 7½, 10, and 11 per cent. Almost ever since we have been in a constant expectation of an invasion, and the depreciation has fluctuated from 9 to 11 or 12 per cent. Hence it appears, that the depreciation cannot be owing *entirely* to general apprehensions of danger, as in that case the depreciation would have ceased at the peace, when those apprehensions must have subsided; but it may be fair to ascribe to them at least the great and sudden rise which took place about the time of the insurrection, and has continued to the present day. I have not the means of inquiring whether the rate of depreciation has corresponded, from time to time, with the amount of the Paper currency, as the Notes of the private Bankers, which are supposed to form so considerable a part of it, cannot be ascertained. If the Specie had left Ireland it would not be difficult to trace so large a quantity in its exit; but it appears to me, from the best inquiries I have been able to make, that much more Specie has been imported into Dublin for these last six or seven years than has been exported from it; and the real rate of Exchange, during that period, having been generally favourable to Dublin, is, in my mind, a proof of the fact; it seems then to follow, that there is or ought to be in Ireland a large quantity of Specie. The practice of hoarding Specie must be greatly facilitated, by the readiness with which Bank Notes can be procured for supplying its place; at present there seems to be no other limitation to the issuing of Notes, than the amount of the good security which the borrowers have to offer for them; and therefore, as all the Bills of the solvent merchants, the public Funds, and the rest of the property of Ireland, as well real as personal, are all good security for borrowing on, Bank Notes issued upon this principle might, by a possibility, be so far extended during a restriction of Specie, that a Paper Guinea (to state an extreme case) might scarcely be exchangeable for a Silver Sixpence. I would wish to add, as to the period when the depreciation commenced, that almost immediately after the suspension Guineas bore a premium of about 2½ or 3 per cent. Specie shops were not opened till some time after, nor was Specie usually sold upon 'Change before the end of the year 1798; prior to this period therefore it is difficult to procure any very accurate account of the depreciation; it began with the colliers requiring Specie to pay for their coals in England; and, I believe, that persons having Specie to dispose of had not at first any market for it, except upon the quays at Dublin.

. . . .

Do you mean, upon the whole of your evidence, to give it as your decided opinion, that the general balance of debt between England and Ireland, including trade remittances, and every pecuniary transaction, has been each year since the restriction on Specie in favour of Ireland?—I do very clearly, except during the two years of scarcity; and upon the whole six years taken together the general balance must have been considerably in favour of Ireland.

Do you also mean, upon the whole of your evidence, to give it as your decided opinion, that there is, and has been, a depreciation in the Paper currency of Ireland, and that the high rates of Exchange which have prevailed, and still prevail, have arisen from that depreciation?—I do; the high Exchange in Dublin, which has now continued for some years, must no doubt have arisen like all other permanently high Exchanges which have ever existed, from the depreciated state of the currency with which Bills of Exchange are purchased, and the same remedy might perhaps be resorted to with success in the present case, which has never failed to be effectual on all former occasions, namely, a removal of the depreciation.

Can you state the causes of that depreciation?—I have already stated to the Committee, that it is partly owing to the peculiar state of Ireland at the present crisis, and partly, I am inclined to think, to an excessive issue of Bank Paper.

On what grounds do you form your opinion that there is an excessive issue of Paper?—From its being depreciated, and not being able to assign any other of the common causes to which I have heard depreciation generally attributed.

What do you mean by the peculiar state of Ireland at this crisis?—The disturbed state of it, and its being threatened with invasion.

How can that operate on the Exchanges, except by producing an increase of remittance of Money from Ireland?—It operates by lessening the value of the Paper currency with which Bills of Exchange are purchased.

Must not the non-residence in Ireland of those Absentees, whose Drafts on Ireland are supposed by some persons to have raised the Exchange, have occasioned a diminished consumption in Ireland of Irish produce and manufactures, and in consequence of such diminished consumption, must there not have existed a greater quantity of Irish produce and manufactures, which Ireland has been able to export?—I apprehend so; I have no doubt that the drains from Ireland by Absentees, however lamentable on other occasions, have had a tendency to force produce out of the country.

Must not the total stock of articles which Ireland has been able to export, have been augmented by the circumstance of the non-residence of Irish Proprietors, nearly in proportion to the amount of the Drafts upon Ireland which those proprietors may be assumed to have drawn?—Probably.

Can you form any opinion what quantity of circulating medium is requisite to carry on the trade and manufactures of Ireland?—I cannot.

Can you form any opinion what quantity of Paper is in circulation in Ireland, including Bank of Ireland Paper, as well as the Paper belonging to the private Banks?—I cannot.

Is it to be understood that the sole reason for your thinking that the issue of Paper in Ireland is excessive, arises from your having stated in a former part of your evidence, that in your opinion the Paper of Ireland is depreciated?—It is the only reason which occurs to me at the present moment.

Do you think the Absentees of Ireland an advantage or disadvantage to Ireland?—I have already stated, that I conceived the money which they draw out of Ireland must have the effect of forcing out produce, and so far favourable; upon the whole, I apprehend the country would derive greater advantages from their living in Ireland.

Do you not think that Ireland could find a foreign market for those articles which are forced out of Ireland by the non-residence of the Absentees?—I am not prepared to answer.

EVIDENCE OF JOHN PUGET

Agent For the Governor and Company of the Bank of Ireland

May 9, 1804. Pp. 125–127

Delivered a duplicate of a continuation of an account of drafts drawn on Messrs. Puget and Bainbridge, from 31st December 1803 to 4th March 1804, and expressed a wish to give a further statement relative to the mode of transmitting the balance of Loans to the Treasury of Ireland.

Witness being accordingly desired to state it, answered, that when a Loan is made in England, of which part is for Ireland, it is then arranged between the Treasuries of England and Ireland, at what periods the proportion for Ireland shall be paid in London, and this arrangement has always been made with the utmost attention to the convenience of Ireland. As soon as those periods of payments are fixed the Lords of the Treasury of Ireland draw Bills on the Paymasters General of England for the Sums, and at the period at which those Sums are to fall due. These Bills the Irish Treasury transmit to their Agents, Puget and Bainbridge, and it was the practice for some time for Puget and Bainbridge (except in a case of emergency) to give the Treasury of Ireland a credit to draw on them only when they had actually received the Money in London, or for Messrs. Puget and Bainbridge, when in Cash, to remit Bills on Dublin to the Bank of Ireland, on the Treasury of Ireland.

That he, from his situation, was well acquainted with the practical part of business, and therefore generally consulted with by the Government of Ireland as to the best mode of transmitting the Loans; he recommended their drawing at twenty-one days sight instead of three days sight, in anticipation of the Bills on the paymasters becoming due. The reasons that he assigned for this change were first, that he observed the Treasury got no allowance in the Exchange from the takers of their Bills for the difference of drawing at three days sight instead of twenty-one days sight. Secondly, that it enabled the Treasury to commence drawing one month sooner, thereby checking the fluctuation in the Exchange by lessening the sum they had to draw on each day, and also extending their periods of drawing. And, thirdly, that should the necessities of Government require the Money to be received in Ireland one month sooner than it is paid in England, it afforded them the accommodation without a charge of interest, and at the same time it did not debar the Treasury of Ireland from drawing at three days, when they had the cash in their Agents hands.

The practice with the Treasury in Ireland in passing their Bills on their Agent in London, appears, from an examination of Mr. Crofton, chief clerk of the Treasury of Ireland, to be as follows:

"In consequence of the great demands by numerous persons for part of the Bills the Treasury had to draw on London, in all cases where those demands could not be complied with, the name of those wishing for Bills were inserted as they made their application, and Bills were given them in rotation;" added to this measure it was determined, as long as the Treasury had but a limited sum to draw, comparative with the demand of the public for their Bills, that no one name of the list should have on any one day more than one thousand pounds British, and to prevent difficulty about the course of Exchange at which their Bills were to be drawn, it was determined that the Treasury should draw only on the day following a regular Exchange day, by which they could fix the course of Exchange of their Bills by the rate of the merchants price on the preceding day.

Much general objection has been raised to the above mode of transmitting the Irish Loans, and insinuations have been thrown out that it afforded partial benefits to some individuals. Every one must admit, as far as regulations went, it is clearly shown that the Treasury used their best endeavours to prevent any partiality in the passing their drafts to London; and though the ingenuity and cunning of man in pursuing his own interest, may sometimes frustrate every check that caution throws in his way, yet, by a reference to the names of those who obtained Bills on London from the Treasury of Ireland, it will appear almost incredible that they should have been distributed with so much impartiality, notwithstanding some persons sent in the names of their clerks and others to obtain Bills for them.

It may be said, that the Agents in London, by their knowledge of the periods at which Government will have to draw, can avail themselves of this foreknowledge, and reap considerable advantages for themselves and their correspondents, by dealing in Exchange at certain periods. The present Agents can prove that neither they nor any of their correspondents have ever benefited by this foreknowledge; nor is it probable that any person of common sense, in the possession of an employ at once so honourable and profitable, would be shortsighted enough to risk the loss of it by pursuing any temporary advantage for himself and others.

An Exchange being against a country has been long held as a proof that the balance of payments was against that country; that is, while the Exchange so remained against her she had more to pay to other countries than to receive from them; but this consolation has always arisen out of an adverse Exchange, that by making the exports of that country cheaper in foreign markets it was an encouragement to exports, and at the same time it was a tax on imports, and thereby discouraged them, and tended to lessen the evil.

Nothing that has been said of late seems to contradict these opinions, and therefore any attempt on the part of the Treasury to lower the Exchange must necessarily prove either disadvantageous or abortive, particularly the latter, as Government can only draw as their occasions require, and their funds in England permit.

It is true, that the Agents in London never remitted a Bill for the Government of Ireland as part of their Loans, at an Exchange under the currency of the day on which they had to remit; their duty was to remit on the best terms, and it would have been even culpable in them to have done otherwise.

The directions they received from the Irish Government were as much as possible to prevent fluctuations in the Exchange; it needs no argument to show, that in the large sums that were to be transmitted to Ireland the Irish Government made no sacrifice of the public property by such conduct, as on the average of the fluctuations the Exchange would have been in all probability the same.

When the amount of the Drafts drawn by the Treasury, and the short periods they were drawn in, are considered, to any impartial commercial man knowing the Dublin market, it will appear astonishing that the fluctuation was so little; and it must be observed, to the credit of those who were employed in the Irish Treasury, that this secrecy alone, respecting the amount to be drawn, prevented the fluctuation that would have occurred, to the loss of the public and the dealers in Exchange.*

There is no doubt but the Treasury would have gained much popularity, possibly even with the importing merchants of Dublin, but certainly with the dealers in Exchange, and with all Irishmen residing in or coming to England, if they had drawn their Bills at par, or at a lower Exchange than the currency; but how they could have justified withholding from the public purse such an advantage without an adequate public benefit remains to be shown.

The English Government in 1800, in conjunction with the Irish Government, agreed to exchange Bank of Ireland Notes at the Bank of

* The following comment is printed in the margin of the Minutes of Evidence, referring to this paragraph:
Exchange was 17 per cent on the 14th of February 1804; from the 3d of March Government drew £.460,000 in nine successive posts, at only £.2.16. per cent on the average of those nine posts, under that price (and the average on what is since drawn is still lower); but in six posts £.400,000, at 3*s.* 6*d.* per cent only, under the quoted rate of Exchange of the preceding day on which they drew.

England, at an Exchange of 9½ per cent to the amount of the instalments due to Ireland, that year; and this was done at the earnest solicitations of some Irish houses in London; but there is reason to suppose that Government did it as an experiment, and from the experience of its partial operation they would not again repeat it.*

By the present mode, the Irish Government have the means of receiving accommodation at an interest of 5 per cent per annum, if their necessities in Ireland should require it, by their Agents in London discounting some of the Bills on the Paymasters, and consequently of the Treasury being remitted, or of the drawing for the amount in advance; and this accommodation on their part of their money raised in England is but reasonable, because they cannot, like the Government of England, issue Exchequer Bills payable out of certain instalments of their Loan to become due.

If it should be determined that the public are not to receive, through the Treasury, the advantage of the Exchange, and that Government are to have the Loans transmitted in future at a fixed Exchange, to the advantage of individuals and the loss of Government, it seems the Treasury, by the regulations they have made, and which are before recited, are as competent to the transacting the business as the Banks of England and Ireland jointly.

But if the Exchange is to be regulated only by the prudence of those employed in transmitting the Loans, then the whole being thrown under the directions of the Courts of Directors of the Banks of England and Ireland, would afford a greater field for individual speculation, and of course of fluctuation, than has been yet practised through the medium of the Treasury of Ireland; and for this plain reason, that notwithstanding the general good intentions and conduct of the Courts of Bank Directors as Courts, yet the periods, and the amount of the sums to be transmitted, being known to twenty-six Directors in England, and eighteen in Ireland, and to twice the number of clerks in both countries, would afford an opportunity to those among them inclined to speculate, without the chance of discovery, that does not exist at present, where it is almost impossible not to fix the charge on those who should be guilty of such a breach of trust.

*A comment is printed in the margin of the Minutes of Evidence, referring to this paragraph:
Government did not at this time receive the notes in Dublin till one month after they were paid in London.

EXTRACT FROM THE BULLION REPORT RELATING TO THE REPORT OF THE IRISH CURRENCY COMMITTEE OF 1804 AND TO THE EXCHANGE RELATIONS OF IRELAND AND ENGLAND

Your Committee must next refer to the confirmation and sanction which all their reasonings receive from the labours of the Committee of this House, which was appointed in a former Parliament to examine into the causes of the great depreciation of the Irish Exchange with England in 1804. Most of the mercantile persons who gave evidence before that Committee, including two Directors of the Bank of Ireland, were unwilling to admit that the fall of the Exchange was in any degree to be ascribed to an excess of the paper currency arising out of the restriction of 1797; the whole fall in that case, as in the present, was referred to an unfavourable balance of trade or of payments; and it was also then affirmed, that "Notes issued only in proportion to the demand, in exchange for good and convertible securities payable at specific periods, could not tend to any excess in the circulation, or to any depreciation." This doctrine, though more or less qualified by some of the Witnesses, pervades most of the evidence given before that Committee, with the remarkable exception of Mr. Mansfield, whose knowledge of the effects of that over issue of Scotch paper, which has just been mentioned, led him to deliver a more just opinion on the subject. Many of the Witnesses before the Committee, however unwilling to acknowledge the real nature of the evil, made important concessions, which necessarily involved them in inconsistency. They could not as practical men, controvert the truth of the general position, that "the fluctuations of Exchange between two countries are generally limited by the price at which any given quantity of Bullion can be purchased in the circulating medium of the debtor country, and converted into the circulating medium of the creditor country, together with the insurances and charges of transporting it from the one to the other." It was at the same time admitted, that the expense of transporting Gold from England to Ireland, including insurance, was then under one per cent; that before the restriction, the fluctuations had never long and much exceeded this limit; and moreover, that the exchange with Belfast, where Guineas freely circulated at the time of the investigation by that Committee, was then $1\frac{1}{4}$ in favour of Ireland, while the Exchange with Dublin, where only paper was in use, was £.10. per cent against that country. It also appeared from such imperfect documents as it was practicable to furnish, that the balance of trade was then favourable to Ireland. Still however, it was contended, that there was no depreciation of Irish paper, that there was a scarcity and consequent high price of Gold, and that the diminution of Irish paper would not rectify the Exchange. "The depreciation of Bank paper in Ireland (it was said by one of the Witnesses, a Director of the Bank of Ireland) is entirely a relative term with respect to the man who buys and sells in Dublin by that common medium; to him it is not depreciated at all; but to the purchaser of a Bill on London, to him in that relation, and under that circumstance, there is a depreciation of ten per cent." By thus avoiding all comparison with a view to the point in issue, between the value of their own paper and that of either the then circulating medium of this Country or of Gold Bullion, or even of Gold coin then passing at a premium in other parts of Ireland, they appear to have retained a confident opinion, that no depreciation of Irish paper had taken place.

It is further observable, that the value of a considerable quantity of Dollars put into circulation by the Bank of Ireland at this period, was raised to 5*s*. a Dollar, for the professed purpose of rendering the new Silver coin conformable to the existing state of the Exchange, a circumstance on which the Committee animadverted in their Report, and which serves to shew that the Irish paper currency could not stand a comparison with the standard price of Silver, any more than with that of Gold Bullion, with Gold in coin, or with the then paper currency of this kingdom.

A fact was mentioned to that Committee on the evidence of Mr. Colville, a Director of the Bank of Ireland, which, though it carried no conviction to his mind of the tendency of a limitation of paper to lower Exchanges, seems very decisive on this point. He stated, that in 1753 and 1754, the Dublin Exchange being remarkably unfavourable, and the notes of the Dublin Bank being suddenly withdrawn, the Exchange became singularly favourable. The mercantile distress produced on that occasion was great, through the suddenness of the operation, for it was effected, not by the gradual and prudential measures of the several Banks, but through the violent pressure which their unguarded issues had brought upon them. The general result, however, is not the less observable.

With a view to the further elucidation of the subject of the Irish Exchanges, which so lately attracted the attention of Parliament, it may be proper to remark, that Ireland has no dealings in Exchange with foreign countries, except through London; and that the payments from Ireland to the Continent are consequently converted into English currency, and then into the currency of the countries to which Ireland is indebted. In the spring of 1804, the Exchange of England with the Continent was above par, and the Exchange of Ireland was in such a state that £.118. 10. of the notes of the Bank of Ireland would purchase only £.100. of those of the Bank of England. Therefore, if the notes of the Bank of Ireland were not depreciated, and it was so maintained, it followed that the notes of the Bank of England were at more than 10 per cent premium above the standard coin of the two countries.

The principles laid down by the Committee of 1804 had probably some weight with the Directors of the Bank of Ireland; for between the period of their Report (June 1804) and January 1806, the circulation of the notes of the Bank of Ireland was gradually (though with small occasional fluctuations) reduced from about three millions to £.2,410,000, being a diminution of nearly 1/5th; at the same time, all the currency which had been issued under the name of Silver Tokens was by law suppressed. The paper currency, both of the Bank of England, and of the English Country Banks, seems during the same period to have gradually increased. The combination of these two causes is likely to have had a material effect in restoring to par the Irish Exchange with England.

The Bank of Ireland has again gradually enlarged its issues to about £.3,100,000, being somewhat higher than they stood in 1804, an increase probably not disproportionate to that which has occurred in England within the same period. Perhaps, however, it ought not to be assumed, that the diminution of issues of the Bank of Ireland between 1804 and 1806, would produce a corresponding reduction in the issues of private Banks in Ireland, exactly in the same manner in which a diminution of Bank of England paper produces that effect on the Country Banks in Great Britain; because the Bank of Ireland does not possess the same exclusive power of supplying any part of that country with a paper currency, which the Bank of England enjoys in respect to the metropolis of the Empire. The Bank of England, by restricting the quantity of this necessary article in that important quarter, can more effectually secure the improvement of its value; and every such improvement must necessarily lead, by a corresponding diminution in amount, to a similar augmentation of the value of Country Bank paper exchangeable for it. That the same diminution for the circulation of private Banks took place in Ireland is more than probable, for the private Banks in Ireland are accustomed to give Bank of Ireland paper for their own circulating notes when required to do so, and therefore could not but feel the effect of any new limitation of that paper for which their own was exchangeable.

APPENDIX 1

BIBLIOGRAPHY OF CONTEMPORARY PUBLICATIONS ON IRISH MONEY, BANKING, AND EXCHANGE 1797–1820

This includes only those publications that deal primarily with the Irish situation, or that have a substantial and organized discussion of it. In addition to the items listed, many publications of the period dealing with the English situation make incidental reference to Irish conditions.

1799

Donoughmore, Lord Viscount. The Substance of a Speech delivered in the Irish House of Lords by Lord Viscount Donoughmore, on Tuesday, 26th of February, 1799. On the Subject of a Bill, introduced by the Earl of Clare, "To restrain the Negociation of Small Notes, and Inland Bills of Exchange, under a Limited Sum." Cork, 1799. Pp. 43.

Also published in a Dublin edition of 54 pages.

1802

[Atkinson, Jasper] Considerations on the propriety of the Bank of England resuming its payments in specie at the time prescribed by the Act 37th, George III. London, 1802. Pp. 110.

[Atkinson acknowledged authorship in a later publication.]

1803

Anonymous. The Bank Note, or Remarks on the Influence Paper Currency has on Society. By an Observer. Dublin [1803] Pp. 24.

[The Royal Irish Academy assigns the date of 1803]

[Horner, Francis] Lord King's Thoughts on the Restriction of Payments at the Banks of England and Ireland. Edinburgh Review. July, 1804. Art. xi.

King, Lord. Thoughts on The Restriction of Payments in Specie at the Banks of England and Ireland. London, 1803. Pp. 106.

The Second edition, enlarged (1804) has the title: Thoughts on The Effects of The Bank Restrictions. Pp. vii and 178.

1804

Anonymous. A Candid Cobler's Cursory and Critical Conjectures on Exchange and Small-Change, on Balance of Trade, on Balance of

Remittance, on Circulating Medium and Kite-Flying. [Presumably published in Ireland.] March and April, 1804. Pp. 46.

Anonymous. Observations on the exchange between London and Dublin. By a merchant of Dublin. Dublin, 1804. Pp. 14.

Anonymous. A Pindaric Epistle: addressed to the Right Hon. Sir Evan Nepean, Bart. occasioned by his letter to the Lord Mayor on the Subject of Bad Silver. Dublin, 1804. Pp. 19.

Anonymous. The Real Causes Of The High Rate of Exchange and The Only True Remedies. Dublin, April 21, 1804. Preface and pp. 78.

Anonymous. A Word of Advice to the trading and monied interests of Ireland, upon the momentous subject of the alarming scarcity of the smaller denominations of silver coin. With some suggestions upon the most feasible mode of regulating the application, of a new coinage, so as to permanently to secure the people of Ireland from a repetition of this calamity. Dublin, 1804. Pp. 25.

Boase, Henry. A Letter to the Right Hon. Lord King in Defense of the Conduct of the Directors of the Banks of England and Ireland. . . . London, 1804. Pp. 52.

Foster, John Leslie. An essay on the principle of commercial exchanges, and more particularly of the exchange between Great Britain and Ireland. London, 1804. Pp. xv and 209.

[Jebb, William, K.C.] An Inquiry into the depreciation of Irish bank-paper, its effects and causes, and a remedy proposed. Dublin, 1804. Pp. x and 93.

[The R.I.A. attributes this to Jebb.]

Magens, Dorrien Magens. An Inquiry into the real difference between actual money, consisting of gold and silver, and paper money of various descriptions. London, 1804. Pp. 68.

Parnell, Henry. Observations upon the state of currency in Ireland, and upon the course of exchange between Dublin and London. London, February, 1804. Pp. viii and 59. Second and 3d. ed., 1804; 4th ed. 1805.

The 4th ed. carries the title: The Principles of Currency and Exchange, Illustrated By Observations Upon the State of the Currency of Ireland, The High Rate of Exchange Between Dublin and London, and the Remittances of Rents to Irish Absentees. Pp. 186.

[Rice, Stephen Edward?]. An argument as to the exchange between England and Ireland; . . . Bath, 1804. Pp. 35.

[The only available copy is in the Seligman Collection at Columbia University, which tentatively assigns the authorship on the basis of an inscription in the pamphlet in a contemporary hand.]

1805

Anonymous. A letter from an Irish member of Parliament, upon the Select Committee of the House of Commons, appointed March 2, 1804, to take into consideration the circulating Paper, the Specie, and the Current Coin of Ireland, and also the exchange Between that part of the United Kingdom and Great Britain. London, 1805. Pp. 52.

[Brinkley, John]. Considerations on the Silver Currency, Relative to both the General Evil as Affecting the Empire, and the Present Enormous Particular Evil in Ireland; With an Appendix containing a Report of Sir Isaac Newton or the State of the Gold and Silver Coin in the year 1717; and also Some Tables relative to the same subject. Dublin, 1805. Pp. 58.

[The copy in the R.I.A. carries the inscription "Dr. Brinkley, T.C.D." The Dictionary of National Biography has a sketch of Dr. John Brinkley, who was an astronomer at Trinity College, Dublin, at this time.]

Lauderdale, Lord. Hints to the Manufacturers of Great Britain, on the Consequences of the Irish Union; and the System since pursued, of borrowing in England, for the Service of Ireland. Edinburgh, 1805. Pp. 51.

Lauderdale, Lord. Thoughts on The Alarming State of The Circulation, and on the Means of Releasing The Pecuniary Grievances of Ireland. Edinburgh, 1805. Pp. 122.

1806

Anonymous. An Essay on the Principles of Commercial Exchanges, and more particularly of the Exchange between Great Britain and Ireland. By John Leslie Foster, Esq. Edinburgh Review. October, 1806. Art. viii.

Payne, D. Beaumont. An exposition of Irish exchange, and other important subjects; being part of a series of letters addressed to the Right Honorable Lord Grenville. City of Wells, 1806. Pp. 84.

[Copies of this book available in libraries in England and the United States have only 84 pages, but an imperfect private copy, purchased in London in 1951, lacks the first 8 pages, is identical on pages 9–84 with the available library copies, and then continues to page 228. It is possible that this is part of a larger volume of more than 228 pages.]

1807

Smith, Thomas. Essay on the Theory of Money and Exchange. London, 1807. Pp. 231. Second edition, 1811. Pp. 248.

1809

Locker, John. Address to The King, The Ministry, and The People of Great Britain and Ireland, on the Present State of the Money System of the United Kingdoms. London. 1809. Pp. xvii and 65.

1810

Anonymous. A short inquiry into the cause of the present distresses of the Irish traders. Dublin, 1810. Pp. 57.

Atkinson, Jasper. A letter to a Member of Parliament; occasioned by the publication of the Report from the Select Committee on the High Price of Gold Bullion. London, 1810. Pp. 108. Second edition, 1811, 104 pp.

1811

Anonymous. A short investigation into the subject of the alleged superfluous issue of bank notes, the high price of bullion, and the unfavourable state of the foreign exchanges: . . . to which is added the substance of the Earl of Rosse's speech in the House of Lords, on the exchange and currency of Ireland . . . London, 1811. Pp. 31.

1812

[M'Donnel, —.] Observations on the present state of the paper currencies of Great Britain and Ireland. Belfast, 1812. Pp. 28.

[The authorship is so given in Halket and Laing, Dictionary of Anonymous and Pseudonomynous English Literature.]

1815

Major, Rev. Henry. Observations Demonstrative of The Necessity to Ireland's Welfare, and to the Character of England, of a Tax upon Absentees; being the substance of four letters to ——. To which is prefixed a letter upon the subject, addressed to the Right Hon. Lord Viscount Castlereagh. Dublin, 1815. Pp. 68.

[Letter to Castlereagh is dated Ballyshannon, March 19, 1812.]

1820

[Symes.] The absentee; or, a brief examination into the habits and condition of the people of Ireland, and the causes of the discontent and the disorganized state of the lower classes. By an officer of the Customs of Ireland. London, 1820. Pp. 42. Dated Dublin, November 4, 1819.

[The authorship is so given in Halket and Laing.]

APPENDIX 2

IRISH EXCHANGE RATES AND SPECIE PREMIUM
1794–1823

1. *Dublin-London Rate in London for 21 day sight bills.*

The "Course of Exchange", a bi-weekly report that had several publishers during this period, gives the rate three times a week. The Irish Currency Report, Appendix (A2) gives the rate three times a week, and quarterly averages, for 1794–March 1804. The Bullion Report, Appendix 66, gives the rate on the first of each month, 1804–March 1810.

Chart 1 is based on the Irish Currency Report for period 1794–1803, and on the "Course of Exchange" for 1804–1823.

2. *Dublin-London Rate in Dublin for 21 day sight bills.*

The Irish Currency Report, Appendix (A1) gives the rate three times a week, and quarterly averages for 1794–March 1804. The Bullion Report, Appendix 66, gives the rate and on the first of each month, 1804–March 1810.

In both 1 and 2, in the periods in which the two sources of data overlap, the figures are identical, or differ only slightly.

3. *Belfast-London Rate in Belfast for 21 day sight bill.*

The Bullion Report, Appendix 68, gives this rate twice a week for the period 1804–1809, although for many individual dates no figures were available.

4. *Dublin-Belfast Rate in Belfast for 61 day sight bills.*

The Irish Currency Report, Appendix (M), gives this rate for the "Beginning" and "Middle" of each month, 1797–April 1, 1804. The Bullion Report, Appendix 68, gives this rate twice a week for the period 1804–1809, for those dates when figures were available.

5. *Newry-London Rate in Newry.* (Presumably for 21 day sight bills).

The Irish Currency Report, Appendix (M), gives the rate, in Specie and in Bank Notes, for the "Beginning" and "Middle" of each month, 1803–January 1804.

6. *Premium on Guineas in Dublin.*

Irish Currency Report, Appendix (L), gives figures, presumably monthly averages, for each month 1799–March 1804. Edward Wakefield (*An Account of Ireland, Statistical and Political.* London, 1812. Vol. ii, p. 206) gives figures approximately twice a month, December 2, 1803–March 2, 1812.

APPENDIX 3

CIRCULATION OF NOTES AND POST BILLS OF THE BANK OF IRELAND 1796–1826

No continuous series is available for the entire period, showing separately Notes and Post Bills. The semi-annual average of Notes and Post Bills combined is available for the entire period, as are quarterly figures for Notes. The principal sources of information are:

1. *Notes on March* 31, *June* 30, *September* 30, *and December* 31, 1796–1825.

   Beginning September 30, 1802 there are separate figures for notes of under £.5, and notes of £.5 and above.

   (F. G. Hall, *The Bank of Ireland,* Pp. 392–394, from the Records of The Bank of Ireland.)

2. *Total of Notes and Post Bills on April* 1, *June* 1, *September* 1, *and January* 1, *January* 1, 1797–*January* 1, 1805.

   (Figure for January 1, 1797 from Journal of The House of Commons. Vol. 59, P. 521, December 13, 1803; for all other dates from Irish Currency Report. Appendix (Z).

3. *Notes and Post Bills on January* 1, *April* 1, *June* 1, *and September* 1, 1805–*January* 1810.

   The note circulation is divided into notes under £.5, and those of £.5 and above.

   (Bullion Report, Appendix 50.)

4. *Average Circulation of Total Notes and Post Bills. Semi-annually, Second half of* 1796—*Second half of* 1822.

   (Bank of Ireland. Accounts Relating to Bank Notes in Circulation, Balances, Unclaimed Dividends, Management of Public Debt, etc. Ordered by the House of Commons, to be printed, 6 May, 1823.)

   Chart 2 is based on the figures in 4.

5. *Average Circulation of Total Notes and Post Bills, Annually,* 1820–1825.

   The combined circulation of Notes and Post Bills is divided between denominations under £.5, and denominations of £.5 and above.

   (Report from the Select Committee on Promissory Notes in Scotland and Ireland. Commons, 1826. Appendix 8).

6. *Note Issues on February* 1 *and August* 1, 1813: *February* 1, 1825.

The Notes are divided between denominations under £.5 and those of £.5 and above.

(Report from The Select Committee on Promissory Notes in Scotland and Ireland. Commons, 1826. Appendix 14.)

7. *Note Issues on May* 1, 1825, *August* 1, 1825, *November* 1, 1825, *February* 1, 1826, *and March* 9, 1826.

The Notes are divided between denominations under £.5 and those of £.5 and above.

(Report from The Select Committee on Promissory Notes in Scotland and Ireland. Commons, 1826. Appendix 13.)

APPENDIX 4

MEMBERS OF THE IRISH CURRENCY COMMITTEE OF 1804*

Mr. Henry Addington
Mr. Henry Alexander
Mr. John Beresford (4)
Mr. John Claudius Beresford
Mr. Nathaniel Bond
Mr. James Brogden
Mr. John Calcraft
Mr. George Canning
Lord Viscount Castlereagh
Mr. Isaac Corry
Lord De Blaquiere
Mr. John Dent
Viscount Henry Augustus Dillion (5)
Lord Viscount Dunlo
Mr. William Elliot
Lord Viscount Folkestone
Mr. John Foster
Mr. Charles James Fox
Mr. Thomas Grenville
Mr. Charles Grey
Lord Archibald Hamilton
Mr. Edward Hardman
Mr. Christopher Hutchinson
Mr. Charles La Touche (4)
Mr. Peter La Touche
Mr. Charles Long
Mr. Mountifort Longfield
Mr. William Manning
Mr. Galway Mills (2)
Mr. Richard Neville
Sir John Newport
Mr. John Patteson (1)
Lord Henry Petty
Mr. William Pitt
Mr. George Ponsonby
Sir William Pulteney
Mr. George Henry Rose
Mr. Charles Shaw (3)
Mr. Richard Brinsley Sheridan
Sir John Sinclair
Mr. Nathaniel Sneyd
Mr. Edward John Stanley (5)
Mr. Robert Steele
Earl Temple
Mr. Henry Thornton
Mr. Samuel Thornton
Mr. George Tierney
Mr. Nicholas Vansittart
Mr. Charles Yorke

All members, unless otherwise indicated, were appointed March 2, 1804. Journal of The House of Commons, Vol. 59. Pp. 129–130.

1. Member appointed March 3, 1804, *Ibid.*, p. 133.
2. Member appointed March 23, 1804, *Ibid.*, p. 173.
3. Member appointed April 27, 1804, *Ibid.*, p. 239.
4. Members appointed April 28, 1804, *Ibid.*, p. 242.
5. Members appointed April 30, 1804, *Ibid.*, p. 246.

* Those whose names are in italics were also members of the Bullion Committee of 1810.

The appointments on April 30, 1804, also include Lord Viscount Dunlo, William Elliot, Lord Archibald Hamilton, and Charles Shaw, all of whom had been appointed originally on March 2, 1804.

It is possible that Edward Lee was also a member of the Committee, although there is no record of his appointment. He stated in a debate in the Commons in 1805 that he had "been a member of the Committee upon Irish affairs" and had "attended carefully to the evidence they produced." Hansard, First Series, Vol. iv, p. 70.

APPENDIX 5

WITNESSES BEFORE IRISH CURRENCY COMMITTEE OF 1804

	Date	*Pages**
Robert Barnewall, Esq. Merchant in London	March 16	49–52
**John Claudius Beresford, Esq. Banker in the City of Dublin	April 17	92–95
Walter Borrowes, Esq. Merchant, at Austin Friars, London	March 6 March 7 March 10 March 16 March 19	23–28 29–32 40 52–53 61–62
William Colville, Esq. Merchant and Director of the Bank of Ireland	April 13 April 14 April 17 April 18 May 4	83–85 85–88 88–90 95–98 118–122
William Coningham, Esq. Merchant in London	March 19	56–58
James Crofton, Esq. Chief Clerk of the Irish Treasury	March 27 March 28	66–70 71
Jeremiah D'Olier, Esq. Director of the Bank of Ireland	April 10 April 12 April 17 April 18 May 1 May 2 May 8 May 9	75 75–78 90–92 96 113–115 115–118 123–124 124–125

* Page references are to the 1826 Commons edition.

** These Witnesses were members of the Committee.

	Date	Pages*
John Finlay, Esq. Banker at Dublin	March 10	40
Thomas Thorpe Frank, Esq. Exchange Merchant of Dublin	April 10 April 20 April 28 May 1	72–75 103 109–112 112–113
Jeremiah Harman, Esq. Merchant	March 10	36–40
John Irving, Esq. Merchant of London	March 20 March 21	58–61 62–66
**John La Touche, Esq. Banker at Dublin	March 10	40
James Mansfield, Esq. Banker in Edinburgh, of the Firm of Mansfield, Ramsey, and Co.	March 8 March 19	32–33 53–56
Robert Marshall, Esq. Inspector General of Imports and Exports of Ireland	April 20 April 24	98–103 104–109
**Sir John Newport Banker in Waterford	March 10 May 8	40 123
John Puget, Esq. Agent for the Governor and Company of the Bank of Ireland	March 5 March 8 March 10 May 9	18–23 33–35 35–36 125–127
John Roach, Esq. Merchant of the City of Dublin	April 12 April 13	78–79 79–83
James Warre, Esq. Merchant in London	March 19	56
Benjamin Winthrop, Esq. Deputy Governor of the Bank of England	March 13 March 14 March 19	40–45 45–49 61

* Page references are to the 1826 Commons edition.
** These Witnesses were members of the Committee.

THE END

GEORGE ALLEN & UNWIN LTD
London: 40 Museum Street, W.C.1

Auckland: Haddon Hall, City Road
Sydney, N.S.W.: Bradbury House, 55 York Street
Cape Town: 58–60 Long Street
Bombay: 15 Graham Road, Ballard Estate, Bombay 1
Calcutta: 17 Chittaranjan Avenue, Calcutta 13
New Delhi: 13–14 Ajmere Gate Extension, New Delhi 1
Karachi: Haroon Chambers, South Napier Road, Karachi 2
Toronto: 91 Wellington Street West
Sao Paulo: Avenida 9 de Julho 1138–Ap. 51

For Product Safety Concerns and Information please contact our EU representative GPSR@taylorandfrancis.com
Taylor & Francis Verlag GmbH, Kaufingerstraße 24, 80331 München, Germany

www.ingramcontent.com/pod-product-compliance
Lightning Source LLC
LaVergne TN
LVHW021111300926
849160LV00009B/697

9781138879829